Creativity – A Sociological Approach

Palgrave Studies in Creativity and Culture

Forthcoming titles:

Marcelo Giglio
CREATIVE COLLABORATION IN TEACHING

Vlad Petre Glăveanu, Lene Tanggaard and Charlotte Wegener (*editors*)
CREATIVITY – A NEW VOCABULARY

Palgrave Studies in Creativity and Culture
Series Standing Order ISBN 978–1–137–44972–6 Hardback
(*outside North America only*)

You can receive future titles in this series as they are published by placing a standing order. Please contact your bookseller or, in case of difficulty, write to us at the address below with your name and address, the title of the series and the ISBN quoted above.

Customer Services Department, Macmillan Distribution Ltd, Houndmills, Basingstoke, Hampshire RG21 6XS, England

palgrave▸pivot

Creativity – A Sociological Approach

Monika E. Reuter

SAGE Institute for Family Development, Boca Raton and The Art Institute of Fort Lauderdale, Fort Lauderdale, United States

palgrave
macmillan

DOI: 10.1057/9781137531223.0001

First published 2015 by
PALGRAVE MACMILLAN

Palgrave Macmillan in the UK is an imprint of Macmillan Publishers Limited, registered in England, company number 785998, of Houndmills, Basingstoke, Hampshire RG21 6XS.

Palgrave Macmillan in the US is a division of St Martin's Press LLC, 175 Fifth Avenue, New York, NY 10010.

Palgrave Macmillan is the global academic imprint of the above companies and has companies and representatives throughout the world.

Palgrave® and Macmillan® are registered trademarks in the United States, the United Kingdom, Europe and other countries.

ISBN: 978–1–137–53123–0 EPUB
ISBN: 978–1–137–53122–3 PDF
ISBN: 978–1–137–53121–6 Hardback

A catalogue record for this book is available from the British Library.

A catalog record for this book is available from the Library of Congress.

www.palgrave.com/pivot

DOI: 10.1057/9781137531223

Contents

Series Editors' Foreword: Socializing Creativity

Creativity has come a long way as a topic of research within the social sciences. From a long-standing fascination with the figure of the genius to being a mental property we all share (at least in potential), there is little ground *within* the individual that creativity scholars did not cover. And yet, despite the individualism intrinsic to many existing models, there is no denying the fact that creativity cannot exist outside of social interaction. Not only are creators using resources from their social context but also the creative act needs the evaluative look of other people for something to be called "creative." This line of thinking, at least in psychology, is known as systemic.

For scholars from other disciplines such as education, organizational studies, and sociology, creativity was systemic from the start. How could we understand students' creativity outside of their interaction with other students, with teachers, with the school environment as a whole? What can we say about the creativity of employees that is abstracted from the context of the group and organization within which they work creatively? Equally, a sociology of creativity could never take its starting point from the isolated individual (as, unfortunately, a lot of psychological literature has done in the past decades). And yet, there is very little written in sociology about creativity, which might come to many as a surprise. Why is this the case?

The long history of individualization of this concept, briefly mentioned earlier, has clearly played a role, going

DOI: 10.1057/9781137531223.0002

hand in hand with its appropriation by psychology. Sociologists might also be wary of a concept that is charged with certain sociopolitical and economic associations. Many creativity discourses are indeed produced to make creative people and their outcomes a commodity. Finally, there is the issue of reification. Creativity as a construct is difficult to place in a sociological frame because it potentially refers to many things at once: people, products, processes, attitudes, beliefs, action orientations, and so on and so forth. How is one to make sense of all of this?

As this thoughtful and vivid analysis of creativity from a sociological perspective demonstrates, we need a strong *sociology of creativity* both for the sake of sociology and for that of the social sciences, including psychology. In sociology, the notion of creativity can be very useful to create a bridge between individuals and society. Indeed, if creative action can never be conceptualized solely as individual *or* social it is because it is simultaneously individual *and* social. This makes it a very interesting analytical concept for a dynamic, relational analysis of the transactions between individuals and their societal context. For the other social sciences, the sociology of creativity brings a renewed interest in the mechanisms of producing *and* validating creativity, more specifically, producing creativity *through* its social validation in a co-constructive act. We are aware today of how group collaboration can shape creative expression. How about institutions, work environments, and technological changes? All these, and more, invite us to consider creativity through a sociological lens.

Monika Reuter's book is a wonderful illustration not only of how a sociological perspective is built, but also of its theoretical and practical consequences. Her review of the field helps one place this view within a larger conceptual landscape. Her empirical work illustrates neatly the construction of creativity within a concrete social setting. But, most of all, her theoretical model is something to be cherished and developed further. One of its great strengths lies in the fact that it bridges traditional gaps between individuals and society, between revolutionary and mundane creations. This is perhaps one of the greatest contributions of a sociological view: it helps us rethink existing categories and articulate them within a broader, more ecological picture creativity.

In the end, creativity itself belongs to no single domain of knowledge or discipline. Nor should it belong to one. Just as creative phenomena are known for their characteristic of crossing boundaries, the study of

DOI: 10.1057/9781137531223.0002

creativity can and should always be *inter- and transdisciplinary* in nature. By adding the voice of sociology to the disciplinary mix, this book decisively contributes to its diversity and creativity.

Vlad Glăveanu
Brady Wagoner
July 15, 2015

DOI: 10.1057/9781137531223.0002

Acknowledgments

Writing this book was an amazing experience: uplifting, humbling, scary at times, and enormously fulfilling. But it is not done alone, even though only my name is on the cover. That means that all shortcomings are mine.

A three-month sabbatical in 2011 from my teaching job at The Art Institute of Fort Lauderdale allowed me to work on the preliminary research for this book, present a paper in France, and give an invited talk at the German Creativity Association.

I owe gratitude to Thomas Luckman who read the chapter on Sociology and gave me critical feedback. Although I cannot agree with his critique of constructionism, I very much benefited from his input and his generosity of sending packets of articles from Switzerland.

Several people reviewed parts of the book and need special mention: Jeff Torlina, Rick Boggs, Maya Shah, and Thomas Reuter. To all of you: thank you. Thank you to my friends in the United States, Kristin Berkey-Abbott, Heather Payne, and my family in Germany, Babs Ziegs and Hartwig Sindt, Mami, Peter and Inge, and Frank and Steffi Muehlhauser, and Wolf Ziegs. This book would not be what it is today without Shefali Shah-Choksi who edited the references and Roslyn Morvay who is an EXCEL expert. My friend Jill Morris is a support system all in and by herself – I'm honored to be a member of SAGE with you.

A very special thank you is due to the editors at Palgrave Macmillan, Eleanor Christie and, especially, Vlad Glăveanu and to Vidhya Jayaprakash at Newgen Knowledge Works, India. Without Vlad's encouragement and guidance, this book would not have been written.

To my husband, David Walczak, and my daughter, Katrina Walczak-Reuter: thank you for your patience.

DOI: 10.1057/9781137531223.0003

About the Author

Monika E. Reuter earned her Bachelor of Science at the University of Maryland, Overseas Division, in Heidelberg, Germany; her Master's at the University of Houston; and her PhD at the State University of New York. She has been teaching Sociology for more than 25 years, and Introduction to Psychology for the past eight years. She serves as the secretary for, and a member of, the Board of Directors of the nonprofit Sage Institute for Family Development in Boca Raton, and has been teaching at The Art Institute of Fort Lauderdale since 2001. She has published on other subjects, but her obsession with the concept of creativity is recent, and unlikely to disappear any time soon. She lives in Fort Lauderdale with her husband and daughter, and several indispensable animals. Comments about creativity are welcome, and should be sent to monika.reuter@gmail.com.

DOI: 10.1057/9781137531223.0004

Introduction

Abstract: *This section introduces the concept of creativity, recounts how the author became initially interested in the concept, and makes an argument for seeing cultural differences when discussing creativity – the cultures across national borders as well as the cultures of different fields (e.g., interior vs. web design).*

Reuter, Monika E. *Creativity – A Sociological Approach.* Basingstoke: Palgrave Macmillan, 2015. DOI: 10.1057/9781137531223.0005.

▶

What do you think when you hear the words "creative" or "creativity"? Art? Children? Genius? Mozart, Van Gogh, or Einstein? The i-phone? What if you were told that the way you think about creativity is shaped by the culture you come from, and those tastes in your lifetime that are presented as "du jour"? What if creativity does not actually exist at all inherently – what if it is merely those products and ideas which are so labeled in our various societies and cultures?

This book is about a concept everybody uses, but that is difficult to define. What is creativity? There are hundreds of definitions in the Western industrialized world, and probably thousands more globally. This book proposes a different way of thinking about creativity, focusing on a sociological explanation where the concept is interpreted as a culture-bound term that is socially constructed. Creativity means something different to an American than it does to a Chinese, and something different to an industrial designer than to a fashion designer. Thus, creativity is a function of fields and domains. All of these individuals live in different cultural contexts, which shape their respective lives and understanding of abstract ideas. Ideas, in turn, are socially constructed.

People do not agree on what creativity is when they look at art, inventions, or products. Societies typically have gatekeepers in every field who tell us what is good and what is not, who gets to be selected for fame, and who does not, who should be celebrated with a cocktail party and a big check. It is *not* the public that selects creativity, it is those knowledgeable in the field who herald the new, the unexpected, the wonderful, the eclectic. That is as true of academics as it is of film directors and interior or web designers. This also implies that the decision on what creativity means tends to be made by a select few in every field of every society.

There are many different interpretations of creativity – all of them chained by, and to, their respective ivory towers. Psychology has traditionally seen people as being creative, while social psychologists and anthropologists have looked at nurturing environments and culture. The bulk of theoretical and research work has been done in Psychology over the past 65 years and there is, interestingly, no formal macro theory of creativity in Sociology, and that is the gap this book seeks to begin to fill.

It is important for me to explain how this book came to be. In August 2009, on my way to work at The Art Institute of Fort Lauderdale (Ai) one morning, I heard a report on WLRN, the local National Public Radio station, about gentrification efforts at Biscayne Boulevard in Miami. A restaurant was mentioned, the Daily Creative Food Company (www.thedailycreativefoodco.com). Creative food? Did this make sense?

DOI: 10.1057/9781137531223.0005

FIGURE I.1   *Creative bread*
Source: Photograph by the author, 2009.

Walking into the restaurant of the Ai to get coffee, I was startled to see the latest bread creations by Culinary students artfully arranged on a large table (Figure I.1). Well, yes, of course ... creative foods!

Now I began to pay attention to how the concept was defined by students at the college, which has the word "creativity" in its mission statement. And yes, of course, it is creative when Industrial Design students construct shoes made entirely out of paper that need to hold their weight. So, do bread and shoes represent creativity?

In order to explore the meaning of the term, focus groups with faculty and students were conducted. One *Research Methods* class which I teach every term helped to construct an open-ended questionnaire asking

DOI: 10.1057/9781137531223.0005

students about their definitions of the concept (N=124). On the basis of those initial responses, two subsequent *Research Methods* classes then designed a survey. The results of this survey were not that surprising until the electronic interviews with employers and industry professionals (e.g., industrial/interior/web/fashion designers, etc.) were analyzed. Comparing the results from those two groups, discussed in Chapter 4, was startling.

In 2011, psychologist Dr. Jill Morris and I organized the annual international meeting of the American Creativity Association in Fort Lauderdale. Over 40 experts gathered on March 30 and April 1, 2011, presenting different approaches on how to research, teach, understand, define creativity. These experts are consultants, or academics with their own businesses, offering various roads to creativity, for example, de Bono's (1985) different colored hats or Black's (1995) use of different crayons. Those ideas represent one explanation in business and innovation, with the assumption that if one uses the right tools, creativity will follow.

This is not, of course, how academics, or artists, or writers with *New York Times* bestseller books, interpret creativity, that is, before his fall from grace, Jonah Lehrer's *Imagine – How Creativity Works* (2012) was hailed as an insight into the concept. Lehrer as well as Malcolm Gladwell (2002a, 2002b) have defined creativity in ways which appeal to the general public, often interchangeably with another concept – innovation.

One way in which the public not only embraces the meaning of creativity, but also perpetuates this interpretation over centuries is to select prime figures who henceforth serve as *the* model creatives or geniuses to be admired. Mozart, for example, and Einstein, Da Vinci, Michelangelo, or van Gogh. In more contemporary times, Steve Jobs comes to mind. Few of those model creatives were female, and all of them are long dead and can no longer take a Torrance test to determine the degree of genius manifest in their personality.

This book proposes a shift in thinking to the idea of socially constructed creativity. Long-held, established belief systems are shaken up by such an approach, that is, the proposition that reality, and thus creativity, are the worlds we construct through our social relationships (Gergen, 2010: viii), and that therefore it does not exist independently suggests that creativity is what we make it to be.

Please note that the book does not include any discussion of art. Art is typically the first thing that comes to mind when discussing creativity, but it is a difficult term that may be even harder to define, and to agree upon, than creativity. Also, interestingly, the concept of art is hardly ever discussed by the domains presented here.

DOI: 10.1057/9781137531223.0005

1
The Concept

Abstract: *Chapter 1 cites numerous examples on how the term "creativity" is used in academic, political, and popular arenas, and various suggestions as to its meaning. The sequence of the chapters that follow is mapped out and their topics briefly addressed, revealing the tremendous schisms across fields and cultures with regard to the meaning of the term. This chapter suggests the debunking of seven common myths and presents a discussion of the shortcomings of one popular 2002 book which has had an impact on American and some international urban development.*

Reuter, Monika E. *Creativity – A Sociological Approach.* Basingstoke: Palgrave Macmillan, 2015.
DOI: 10.1057/9781137531223.0006.

Why, asks Hargadon (2004), is creativity still such a fascinating, yet elusive, concept after decades of study? The term, believed to have been coined in its present interpretation in 1927 by Alfred North Whitehead (1978), is used in daily life, from politics (i.e., President Obama's 2011 State of the Union address, German Chancellor Angela Merkel's speech at the 2006 World Economic Forum, and Rahm Emanuel's 2013 call for action to fix America's dire infrastructure problems) to television shows such as the *Food Network* in the United States. In 2009, the European Commission declared an official *Year of Creativity and Innovation* even though practical outcomes of that effort are hard to quantify, and useful outcome is one criterion often applied to defining or measuring creativity in the Western world. During a speech in February 2015, German cultural minister Gruetters revealed that there are 250,000 organizations in the creativity industry with over 1 million employees and an estimated annual revenue of 145 billion euros in the European Community (2015). Ergo: Creativity matters, especially economically.

The term "suffers from inflationary overuse" (McEwan, 1998) in the public sphere while at the same time it is defined domain-specifically (see next chapter) in academia. Deeply embedded first in Psychology and more recently in Social Psychology, it has found its way into a variety of other fields, even spawning an entire consulting industry – but there still is no consensus on its meaning. As Geertz said, creativity is one of the "big words," that is, a grand concept that is often used, but hardly ever defined adequately (in Adolf et al., 2013). There are medical models, for example, the study of brain wave changes during the creative thinking process (Shiu et al., 2011), measuring alpha and beta power, as well as a biological one (see Reuter et al., 2005). More recently, with advances in technology in the medical world, there are also increasingly neuroscientific investigations, especially about the possibility of fostering creativity (Waytz and Mason, 2013).

In one segment of the US popular science television show *Through the Wormhole* (Discovery Channel, undated), a creativity cap was introduced which supposedly is capable not only of detecting where creativity resides in the brain, but also, by administering short electrical currents, changing the way in which people come up with answers to puzzles much more creatively. Similarly, English (2011) reports on a research study engaging a "Thinking Cap" that was supposed to promote creativity in 213 undergraduate students.

Alternatively, it has been closely linked to the need of using new computer technologies, that is, according to Resnick (CHI Conference,

2009), these have the potential to aid people become creative thinkers living in a creative society, leading to, as the United Nations specifies in its 2013 Human Development Report, "entrepreneurial creativity and social policy innovation" worldwide (United Nations, 2013). Another example for a different conception of the term is Rettig's (2010a, 2010b) proposition that especially one precondition needs to be fulfilled for creativity: leisure! He also insists that if the "right" people in the "right" environment are being managed in the "right" way, innovations will almost certainly follow. Employees need to feel that their employers support innovative thinking, which will lead to more overall creativity (translation mine). For Zimmer (2001) all that good new products need are businesses devoted to enabling their employees' potential (translation mine). Tanner (1997) echoes this sentiment and proposes "total creativity in business" but for Oelze (2012), creativity is the demystification and democratization of the modern concept of genius. Creativity, in his view, has become a criterion for achievement that everybody is supposed to fulfill (2012, translation mine).

Krämer (2012: 111–112) suggests that the creative and self-organized employee is a role model for successfully working and acting in our current society. Moreover, "creativity is an expression of happiness in politics, a euphemism of the new capitalism, and a healing slogan of modern culture" (Hentig in Oelze, 2012: 79, translations mine). Creativity has become a central job and life skill, even though there is no solid explanation of its meaning, and it certainly is difficult to "hire for creativity" (Inc. Guidebook, 2010). Csikszentmihalyi (cited by Tanggaard, p. 126, in Glăveanu et al., 2015) thus says that creativity "is no longer a luxury for the few, but a necessity for all" and Oelze (2012: 82, translation mine) finds that "Creativity is whatever people think of when they speak about it!"

What deserves to be called creative? Valsiner et al. (2015) make this interesting observation: "The warm sun, or the full moon, are not to be given the honor of being creative – even as the sunrays are crucial to the upkeep of our natural survival" (p. xviii). Certain processes, products, and people are called creative, and as of the second half of the last century, even corporations, countries, economies, cities, social classes, and milieus (Merkel in Oelze, 2012: 81–82, translation mine). Habitus forms so that many social areas are suffused by the logic of the total creative imperative, say Kurt and Göttlich (2012: 10), which means an epidemic expansion of a creativity norm in Western societies. In the public, this conception of creativity is often regarded as "a theological,

DOI: 10.1057/9781137531223.0006

if not metaphysical concept of a miracle" (2012: 10). Florida (see the discussion later in this chapter) reserves the label for people – young, hip, technologically sophisticated with a flair and desire for rock music and specific urban areas. If they are also gay, creativity seems to turn into an automatic outcome for any city willing to spend money on the developments he recommends.

What just these few examples illustrate is how many different definitions and interpretations there are for the concept of creativity. A brief literature review on creativity from ten different academic domains is presented in Chapter 2: (1) organizational studies; (2) everyday and social creativity; (3) innovation; (4) creativity as a function of groups; (5) creativity as intelligence; (6) creativity as a by-product of madness in psychopathology; (7) creativity in education; (8) chaos/philosophy/ design fields; (9) commercial consulting; and (10) psychology. Chapter 3 maps out a theory of creativity from a sociological perspective and presents a model that seeks to explain the social construction of creativity. Chapter 4 reports the results of an ongoing longitudinal triangulation research project which started out by asking students and then employers and industry professionals what creativity means to them. The concluding chapter lays out the major shortcomings of the present research and future research questions.

Even though there are mostly open questions (is creativity innate? can it be learned? what would be the best approach to teaching it?), an entire industry in Western industrialized societies teaches creativity. Consulting firms have arisen around the concept, and associations link themselves to the idea (the American Creativity Association, the German Creativity Association [Deutsche Gesellschaft fuer Kreativitaet], the French Creativity Association [CREA]). Creativity in this domain is often considered the basis for innovation or for better corporate management. Here, it can be learned and it can be taught. In addition, thousands of books have been published on how to learn to be more creative in one's own life.

Education and creativity are closely linked, that is, there are a variety of interpretations of the significance of creativity in education (see domain 7). Edward de Bono insists that creative thinking is first and foremost a question of discipline (Tönnesmann, 2009, translation mine). Everybody can learn creativity, just as everybody can learn how to play tennis. He criticizes educational systems that have imprinted in us the logical thinking models of Plato, Sokrates, and Aristotle who developed

DOI: 10.1057/9781137531223.0006

a thought system that depends on analyses and judgments. For 2,000 years, de Bono says, schools and universities have used this system as their mantra, which means we know many different and excellent ways to find truth, but only a few ways to create new thinking (in Tönnesmann, 2009, translation mine). The biggest problem today, according to him, is not climate change, wars, or crises, but poor, uncreative thinking (in Tönnesmann, 2009, translations mine). Sir Robinson (2001), one harsh critic of the present Western educational system, agrees with de Bono and also believes that creativity can be learned, while Makel (2009) asks creativity researchers to help bring creative thinking into the classroom.

Some experts believe creativity to be "our true human nature" (Fox, 2004) as others claim that it grows around diversity (Florida, 2002) or see it as "essential to the existence of humanity" (Vygotsky in Lindqvist, 2003: 249). A number of scholars, gurus, and journalists regard creativity as a unique gift, eminence, or genius (see Riedemann, 2011, translation mine) while others grant it everyday status, acknowledging that all people, throughout their lives, have the capacity for creativity (domain 2, Ruth Richards, 1999a, 1999b, 2007).

The field gets further muddled by very different assumptions about creativity's importance. In the German science magazine *GEO*, for example, Langer (2011, translations mine) describes how crucial it is to develop "fantasy" in children. He argues that the royal discipline of homo sapiens is not intelligence, but role play – the stage where children practice to become human. That is an ability, Langer claims, which is only accessible via creativity. The play of children is equivalent to foreign trips – imagining what could be behind the borders of reality. Age, he asserts – and both social psychologists and sociologists would add, cultural imprinting during socialization! – prevents adults from seeing the magical. Langer also presumes that abiding by rules and norms kills creative capacity as we age (translation mine). Even very young children already seem to be impacted by variations in culture. Interesting here is a project by the University of Osnabrück, cited in Langer's article, which compares drawings of children from around the world. The drawings reflect the cultural differences from one society to another, even though the subject of the task, that is, illustrating "family," was the same. The research concludes that children see the world very differently as a result of the culture in which they have grown up.

Creativity has been both called a god-given gift and equated to madness (see domain 6) whereas authors in domain 4 see creativity

DOI: 10.1057/9781137531223.0006

as originating from group efforts, and some in domain 5 consider it a by-product of intelligence. In domain 8, creativity is part of chaos, and in the field of Sociology, described in Chapter 3, the concept has been almost completely ignored.

There are hundreds, and globally probably thousands, of definitions: Aleinikov et al. (2003) furnish 101, mostly by everyday people and artists, while Treffinger (2000) supplies 112, predominantly from academic environments. Also noteworthy is Isaksen's (2008) compendium of creativity definitions with extensive bibliographic reviews. In the context of the *World Creativity and Innovation Week,* the HR's Workplace Learning and Development Team, the AU Innovation Facilitators, and the Center for Teaching, Research and Learning (American Education, undated) published 75 quotes about creativity and innovation. Andersson and Sahlin (1997) have called this multitude of interpretations the "complexity of creativity."

Then there is also the question of whether creative capacities are being lost, and what it means for adults when they have been defined as creative while they were children. Bronson and Merryman (2010) have reported on the amazing predictability potential of Torrance's test with the 400 "Torrance Kids" in an ongoing longitudinal study, begun in 1958. The study investigates their accomplishments as adults. Bronson and Merryman come to an interesting conclusion in this article, that is, the Flynn effect with intelligence quotients in international comparisons. IQ scores are going up by ten points annually because of increasingly enriched environments. The opposite is true for the Torrance creativity scores, that is, in the United States, those have been falling since approximately 1990. See also, for this argument, Kim's analysis of 300,000 US children's creativity tests (2007) and LiveScience's (2011) question why US children are becoming less creative. The decline is seen as most serious for younger children from Kindergarten to sixth grade. So, if creativity is lost, what can be done to get it back? That question has yet to be researched.

A look across domains and fields presented here reveals tremendous schisms in the use of the term where meanings are often contradictory. And yet, very few of the domains described consider cross-cultural interpretations of creativity (Raina, 1999), or how the term is perpetuated especially in the public. Creativity is analyzed in this volume not as a product, an action, or a personal talent, but as an effect of specific arrangements of social practices (Passoth, 2012). This also means that both academics and the public should discard the following widespread myths:

1   that creativity is innate and person-specific (Mozart and Einstein were creative, but Ms. Jones and Mr. Smith are not). The persistent belief in the individual genius who is different, with god-given ideas, is misplaced from a sociological perspective. See, as an example of this very common belief system, economist Galenson who describes "the contributions of those rare individuals who can make a huge difference in science, technology and business" (2006: 30);

2   that creativity is not only a gift bestowed on only a few, but that it also does not need to be practiced. Creativity means persistence, work, concentration, passion, and the need for new knowledge along the way, as creatives will advise;

3   that all you need to exercise creativity is free time, that is, Rettig's (2010b, translation mine) argument that the one precondition especially important for creativity is leisure;

4   that children are still "naturally" creative while adults have lost it. Children's play does not lead to innovation, or new ideas. It is pure fantasy. Even the most creative kids do not have to compete for the best ideas, or have to be concerned about earning paychecks by innovating products. In addition, some adults who can play at work may be subjected to harsh demands by their bosses (a well-known example is Steve Jobs). Despite media stories every once in a while of a child displaying incredible artistic talents, Mozarts or Einsteins do not typically come in mini versions;

5   that creativity is the same around the world;

6   that creativity is male – either it is inherently male, or it is inherited by males from their fathers. During an interview, British musician and songwriter Omar Lye-Fook (National Public Radio, 2013), for example, said that music is in his blood because his father was a drummer with Bob Marley and the Rolling Stones. However, creativity has not (yet!) been found to be a paternal genetic predisposition;

7   that creativity is connected to money or usefulness. For many people, if an idea doesn't translate into a dollar, it is not creative in the first place.

Apart from deconstructing these ideas, does environment matter as much as, or less or more than genius or talent? Is economist Cowen

(2013) correct when he suggests that the secure life in US middle classes, that is, "average," is over – or do most people have a very different future ahead, one with excitingly creative careers, as a popular book suggested for the 21st century? When Richard Florida published *The Rise of the Creative Class* in 2002, accolades about his predictions abounded. Yet ten years later, those predictions have not come true.

Why discuss Florida in this book? He has had a tremendous impact on US urban development as both small and big cities have embraced his ideas of creative places. Critiques of Florida address additional issues. While he sees an ascendance of the creative class in America as a positive development which should be actively supported both socially and politically, Peck (2005) furnishes a searing criticism of the bifurcation of hedonistic creatives and the "Lumpen two-thirds" (p. 757).

Florida's idealistic vision of a creative knowledge society and the rise of creative classes, that is, "people who are paid principally to do creative work.. scientists, engineers, artists, musicians, designers and knowledge-based professionals" (2002: xiii) has not become reality in the United States. One reason for this failure can be found in his definition of the work he considers creative. Just because he classifies occupations into a creative class does not mean that people in these jobs would consider their work creative, that is, "that they also get to do more enjoyable work and they contribute more by *adding creative value* (that's why they are paid highly)" (Florida, 2002: xv). Labor specialists would disagree that this switch-over to a creativity-driven economy where people love their job and get paid well has indeed occurred. Cowen's 2011 *The Great Stagnation* and his 2013 *Average Is Over* (both *New York Times* bestsellers) describe a very different reality in the world of work of contemporary America, and that reality is strikingly unlike Florida's vision.

Kotkin (2013) cites Florida as conceding the limits of his creative class vision, which includes admitting that the trickle-down benefits which he foresaw have not actually taken place. His predictions have come true for a limited segment of the young, hip population, and for cool districts in some urban areas, but have done little, if anything, to elevate the economic or creative status of the middle or working classes (p. 3).

Other critics of creative class visions are equally acerbic, among them German sociologist Oelze (2012) who sees a new "creativity cult" because the idea of creativity is in such stark contrast to the lives of people in a bureaucratized world (p. 88, translation mine). Florida's idea fits Western ideologies of individualism and fashions consumerism, and

DOI: 10.1057/9781137531223.0006

it fits the ideal of free work where new job types are in contrast to jobs of the postindustrial service economy. These types of jobs, Oelze says, are no longer seen in the traditional sense of the working classes, but as expressions of creativity (p. 88, translation mine) and behind this euphemism is hidden serious economic interest, and increased expectations of performance demand in a cold, hysterically accelerated society (p. 89, translations mine).

Not only are the economics behind Florida's theories incorrect (Malanga, 2004), but his basic argument is tautological, that is,

> So, growth derives from creativity and therefore it is creatives that make growth; growth can only occur if the creatives come, and the creatives will only come if they get what they want; what the creatives want is tolerance and openness, and if they find it, they will come; and if they come, growth will follow. (Peck, 2004: 757)

Florida's assumption that hair salon, construction and landscaping, or spa work "is already creative work" (2002: xv) is also problematic. It is certainly true that "relegating vast numbers of people ... (who)... do rote work is a dreadful waste of human capabilities" (Florida, 2002: xvii), but the research reported in Chapter 4 of the current book indicates, contrary to Florida's predictions, that even employers in so-called creative fields are more interested in good little working ants than people with creative minds. Those who pay for the labor of others – even in design fields – want reliable work, not birthing of great ideas by super-creative prima donnas.

Florida has been called "the relocation agent for the global bourgeoisie" (Whyte, 2009: 1) as his ideas are being spread around the world. Moreover, many of the "creative cities" on Florida's index list have been shown not to do very well economically today (see Malanga, 2004). Peck (2004) accuses Florida of "amateur microsociology" (p. 744) and questions the idea that the economic function of creatives makes them "the natural – indeed the only possible – leaders of 21st Century society" (p. 745), including Florida's barber who owns a BMW, and his housecleaning lady whose husband drives a Porsche. Inequality? Growing poverty? Low-wage jobs? Job security? Benefits that employees can rely on? Those issues are not addressed.

Thompson (2002) describes an interesting example of a so-called creative field in which Florida's predictions have not come true. Programmers, Thompson finds, notice mistakes in corporate databases but do not correct them because, as a programmer explained, "I would tell them if they weren't about to make money off me" (2002: 3). Florida's vision of a corporate system that enhances and fulfills the creative needs of its workers is not the reality for Thompson's programmers. In addition, the mushrooming of web open source research, design, and innovation serves as another example of the move of creative work away from Florida's envisioned happy creative class and benevolent employers.

Florida selected three Ts, that is, talent, technology, and tolerance for constructing an overall Creativity Index. The interpretation of creativity in the current book has nothing to do with three Ts or happy creatives but instead focuses on how meanings of what is or is not creative are socially constructed, that is, there simply is no creativity unless a group of influential people agrees that it is. Florida did not address this issue either.

Florida was wrong in figuring out how to grow economies. US society has not, during the past ten years, made "massive investments in creativity (such as in higher education, scientific research and culture),... by drawing waves of energetic, intelligent people from all over the world" (2002: xxiii), and his concern about competition from other countries was misplaced. The countries he predicted to be the future economic winners in the global competition for creative ideas, that is, Finland, Sweden, Denmark, the Netherlands, Ireland, Canada, Australia, and New Zealand all face economic woes today – along with Greece, Italy, and Spain, which have been teetering on the verge of financial collapse. Far from having become economies that are growing because of creativity, the last three countries have been fighting for economic survival while negotiating with the European Community for help.

Florida's predictions were wrong because everyday life in the United States has not been transformed due to a creative economy. The new creative social class he saw on the horizon has not emerged, and creativity has not become the "fundamental source of economic growth" (p. xxix). The US government no longer has the money to adequately fund higher education, which has increasingly been left to private entities, corporations in both non-, and for-profit education. There have been problems, however, so that, for example, the Obama administration's concern with "Gainful Employment" has begun to impact higher education institutions. Also affected are publishing companies in the United States that have branched out into online or classroom applications such as *MyMath*

Lab by Pearson. Creativity? According to Sir Robinson (2010), that has been left in the dust long ago in schools.

Another problem with Florida's predictions is his definition of the creative class which contains many occupations which sociologists of work would classify as the service industry. He counts too many occupations, often occupations with vastly different educational requirements (hair dresser vs. scientist) and occupations with vastly different incomes, as members of the creative class. The glorious future Florida painted for educators in 2002, for example, has not become a reality. Adjuncting has been the norm for most college professors in the American educational system which is experiencing an earthquake, shaking up academics' lives. The country is deeply in debt, that is, more than $18 trillion (US National Debt, May 2015), and relief has not come from a politically divided Congress. Where are Florida's creative classes that are supposed to pull the country out of its economic slump?

Yet, Florida believed that creativity is the ultimate economic resource, even as discussions continue over the disappearance of the middle classes in the United States and which segments of the stratified society gain the most financially. Florida's book touched on some very interesting and important issues: the diversification of the labor force and the ranking of different cities in the United States as more or less open to, and facilitating, creativity. But overall, in his glowing predictions for the future, and vision of a society in which the creative ethos reigns supreme, Florida was incorrect.

What, then, does creativity mean to a society, to labor, to people? The chapter that follows takes a look at different ways in which the concept has been defined.

DOI: 10.1057/9781137531223.0006

2
Ten Domains That Have Explained Creativity ... Or Maybe Not

Abstract: *Chapter 2 introduces the ten prominent domains in creativity research and theory from the past decades. Arguments are presented from (1) organizational studies; (2) everyday and social creativity theories; (3) the innovation field that lays claims to creative roots and manufactures new products and designs, as well as ideas of creativity rescuing the American economic system; (4) the idea that creativity originates in groups; (5) the theory of the correlation, if not causal relationship, between creativity and intelligence; (6) the psychopathology field where it is assumed that creativity and genius are closely connected to madness; (7) the education field that proposes that creativity can be taught; (8) chaos theory/economic theory/the philosophy of creativity/design thinking/bio-mimickry/social creativity, each of which determines creativity as originating from a different source; (9) the commercial consulting industry that proposes that creativity can be learned; and (10) the domain of psychology.*

Reuter, Monika E. *Creativity – A Sociological Approach*. Basingstoke: Palgrave Macmillan, 2015. DOI: 10.1057/9781137531223.0007.

DOI: 10.1057/9781137531223.0007

The following ten domains represent vast differences in the use of the concept of creativity, especially cross-culturally, suggesting that although creativity can be found all around the world, it cannot be globally defined. Instead, definitions are formulated, changed, and served up as needed so that being creative means different things across cultures, fields, and especially people. Creativity is, by definition, universally social because there is no opposition between the individual and society in an atomistic way (termed "methodological individualism" by Purser and Montuori, 2000) – neither individual nor society can exist without the other, and neither is possible without creativity.

Domain 1 focuses on organizational studies, the "foundation for corporate success" (Pfohl, 2010: 105). Amabile and Gryskiewicz (1989) investigate stimulants and obstacles in work environments via the Work Environment Inventory (WEI), and Amabile et al. (1996) continue that work of determining creativity in organizations by introducing the KEYS (formerly: WEI) scale built on psychometric characteristics. The focus in these two studies is on the validity and reliability of the scales, not the prevalence of creativity.

Amabile's earlier work (1982, 1983a, 1983b) deals with the social-psychological aspects of creativity in organizations, that is, innovation as outcome in social environments that support creative behavior. Sennet, in his book about the history of craft, talks about the powers of imagination (2008: 10) fueling technological understanding. He acknowledges the role of society in divorcing technical knowledge from creativity by "sort(ing) people along a strict gradient of ability" (p. 268). This represents the notion of organizational creativity as embedded in a few, specific, special people in contemporary popular understandings of the concept. Hage, on the contrary, reviews variables that influence organizational innovations, and calls the complexity of the division of labor the most important one "because it taps the organizational learning, problem-solving and creative capacities of organizations" (1999: 597; 2007).

Differences between managers and nonmanagers and males and females with respect to perceptions of organizational climates bring the discussion back to the individual level (Kwasniewska and Necka, 2004). Remaining with this individual focus, Kirton (2003) who developed the *KAI inventory* to gauge problem definition and problem-solving styles of individuals aims his approach at managers and academics, but also points out that it is limited to individuals' "preferred thinking styles" in organizations.

DOI: 10.1057/9781137531223.0007

Leavy asserts that "business organizations are under pressure to become more creative ... in everything they do" (2003: 51), and to achieve this goal, they have to become more hospitable to "unusual ideas and people." Creativity, he promises, will also bring a bonus in the form of a breeding ground for leaders. He insists that "out-of-the-box" ideas are least likely to come from "in-the-box" people, so businesses have to learn to tap their employees' creative potential and embrace the unusual people among them. It is "the unusual" people for Leavy, who bring the creative edge.

Ekvall investigates the influence of the organization on workers' capacity to be creative (1993, 1996, 1997, 1999, 2000), that is, on engineers' perception of control versus freedom in creative work (1993), on differing influences of higher and lower level creativity in organizations as measured by the earlier-mentioned KAI scale, and employing the four Ps of creativity, that is, product, person, process, and press (originated by Rhodes, 1961). Ekvall develops a "Creative Climate Questionnaire" (1996), an instrument that measures organizational structure and climate for creativity and innovation – not workers' perceptions.

A very different view of modern management ideology is presented by Oelze (2012) who says that even the lowest workers are nowadays pressed to display creativity and originality. This partially derives, he argues, from our insufficient understanding of creativity (especially in the work environment), which is a relatively new phenomenon because its emergence and high relevance are a result of recent developments in economics and society (p. 84, translation mine).

On the organizational theory side, Hall (1987) describes innovation as a significant departure from existing practices – be they in technology or organizations (e.g., management tools). They are distinguished by radicalness, and Hall describes 19 characteristics that are of importance in adaptation (pp. 206–208) and elaborates on the organizational characteristics that make innovation possible. It should be noted, however, that he declares that "innovation is viewed as a political process" () because of the crucial importance of the environment.

__Domain 2__ discusses "everyday creativity" and "social creativity." Everyday creativity, broadly speaking, is the label for the view that everybody, every day, engages in creative problem solving (see Ruth Richards, 2007). Glăveanu distinguishes between the "we paradigm" of social creativity, the "he" paradigm of the genius and the individual "I-type paradigm ... asserting that every person has a creative potential;

this potential can be developed and is not purely innate; and creativity is specific to everyday life and not 'reserved' exclusively for artists or scientists" (2010: 149). This way of thinking argues for a democratization of creativity so that creativity belongs to everybody. The emphasis is a marriage of the individual with the social factors that enable creative processes. A similar argument for taking into consideration both the individual and the environment is made by Purser and Montuori with the proposition of "a more contextual framework" (2000).

Everyday creativity concerns everyday people who engage in creative endeavors. Here, the individual is welded with her social environment and her capacities for problem solving in that social environment. Thus, Sarah Richards describes "red-hot eco moms" who create different designs for eco-friendly solutions to everyday problems (i.e., diapers, reusable gift wrap, music, nontoxic toy cleaner, a smarter lunchbox) (undated). This mirrors what Flora says, "Just because you'll never be Brando or Balanchine doesn't mean that you can't harness your idea-generating powers and make your life your own masterpiece" (2009: 1). How people engage in creativity not only in their everyday life, but even in unusual circumstances is detailed by Flora. She reports on Russian prisoners who are neither trained painters nor have proper equipment, but who design and then create amazing tattoos. This is not Einstein's relativity theory, or Mozart's *Eine Kleine Nachtmusik*, but pertains to the daily creative lives of people, or how people use creative thinking in their daily lives.

Ruth Richards argues that all people, throughout their lives, have the capacity for creativity (1999a, 1999b). One discovers creativity not just in special cognitive achievements, but also in many daily behaviors, insists Brodbeck (2006). "Almost anyone under almost any circumstance can be creative," says LaChapelle (1983: 132), and Ruth Richards laments that in conventional thinking, "creativity is about arts, or maybe sciences, or at least about special fields of endeavor. Sometimes it is about special people as well, such as famous artists, best-selling novelists, or ground-breaking scientists ... Such creativity is not primarily about us. Everyday creativity is about everyone, throughout our lives; it is fundamental to our survival" (2007: 25).

Solidifying the arguments of the everyday creativity proponents, Sawyer et al. (2003) say that creativity is everywhere human imagination combines, changes, and makes anything. In addition, the product of creativity is not as important as the gatekeepers of the domain. Thus, learning the rules and content of the domain and the field, the criteria for

DOI: 10.1057/9781137531223.0007

selection, and the preferences and problems of the field would constitute good training for creativity (Csikszentmihalyi, 1996: 47–48). Creativity is not only "essential to the existence of humanity and society, but also necessary for our process of consciousness" (Vygotski in Lindqvist, 2003: 249). Pfütze (2012: 251) agrees that mini and pop creativity are meant to strengthen the quality of life, that is, everybody has a talent which merely needs to be awakened and nurtured – whether it be karaoke or baking cakes (translation mine). This has also been referred to as "little c" creativity (Kersting, 2003).

In order not to be strapped down by the notion of "art," Jefferson (2001) argues that "our own creativity can spur us on – to look for a different way to work or find our way through a struggle with someone we love" (p. 212). She cites the civil rights movement, the antiwar movement of the 1970s and the women's and gay rights movements as examples of creative periods in cultures. Chambers (2001) challenges our seeing as creative only those things that have become successful: she wants us to find joy in doing things – even if we do them badly. Thus, she declares, "chocolate doesn't have to be beautiful to taste good" (p. 219).

Other everyday creativity proponents also reject the idea that creativity is something affixed to what we commonly call "art." The Root-Bernsteins (2008) are part of that chorus, as are Moreau and Dahl (2009). Too often, the implication is that money or fame is the only indicator of creativity. What is different in the literature on everyday creativity is the notion that creative endeavors are not just a unique talent of a few genius heads who produce monumental new things. Here, the nod is to everybody who makes life easier, or who finds a solution to problems which people (such as parents) encounter on a daily basis. This necessitates discussing the concept of innovation, which is often believed to be different from creativity.

  Domain 3 introduces the concept of innovation which refers to new products as outcomes of creative thinking. Apart from Alexander Graham Bell or Benjamin Franklin, we as a public are usually ignorant of the heroes of contemporary innovation such as Sir Tim Berners-Lee and his colleagues at CERN who invented the World Wide Web and gifted it to the world; Marty Cooper (*The Economist*, 2009), the father of the cell phone, who was also instrumental in establishing high-capacity paging, and in popularizing the Quarts Watch, and Ajay Bhatt, an INTEL fellow, who coinvented the USB with Dov Moran (Glass and Knight, 2013). These are the people who revolutionize our daily practical lives.

DOI: 10.1057/9781137531223.0007

In Europe, during the 2009 *Year of Creativity* (European Commission, 2009b), creative industries were called worldwide guarantors of growth and the homes of knowledge societies. But Reck (2008) criticizes propositions that creative classes will swoop in and save the future of the world. He observes that the type of creativity that leads to innovation also leads to a conventional amassing of things and reaffirms values typical for individualistic and technologized Western industrial societies. He proposes that real innovation would consist of making possible the self-organization of well-educated and engaged lay people resulting in extreme changes of knowledge (translation mine).

During a presentation at the German Creativity Association (Reuter, 2011a), its members insisted on a sharp separation between the terms "Kreativitaet" and "Innovation." While the terms were not specifically defined, the association (Deutsche Gesellschaft fuer Kreativitaet) published its yearbook under the auspice of innovation (Preisz, 2010), and a volume dedicated to Horst Geschka, the "Herr Creativity of Germany" (Parnes, 2010) is titled *Always one idea ahead: how innovative corporations utilize creativity systematically* (Harland and Schwarz-Geschka, 2010, translation mine). Markman and Wood (2009a) also suggest that innovation is going to save our economy, and that being creative means using old ideas in new clothing called "analogy" (see also Markman et al.; Weisberg et al.; Tversky and Suwa; Smith et al.; Ward et al.; Summers et al.; Bridewell, all in Markman and Wood, 2009b).

A much more negative view of the significance of creativity is proposed by Bronson and Merryman who write about "the creativity crisis" in the July 19 edition of *Newsweek* and lament that American creativity is declining, especially in children (2010). Vaclav Smil goes as far as to declare that "the demise of U.S manufacturing dooms the country not just intellectually but creatively, because innovation is tied to the process of making things" (Thompson, 2013: 72). Innovation is needed to pull America out of its current economic troubles – the question is just, how to do it. Opposition to that view is furnished by Gimmler who criticizes "the creative industry's... reductive understanding of creativity as innovation" (2006: 5).

Catmull, cofounder and President of Pixar and Disney Animation Studios (2013, personal e-mail exchange with Pixar), says in the *Harvard Business Review* (2008) (henceforth abbreviated as HBR), that there is a "misguided view of creativity that exaggerates the importance of the initial idea in creating an original product" (p. 65). Pixar creates all

DOI: 10.1057/9781137531223.0007

stories, worlds, and characters internally with a community of artists. It adheres to sets of principles and practices for managing creative talent and risk, and its creativity process involves large numbers of people from different disciplines working together. HBR picks up the subject of innovation again in July–August 2011 where Ibarra and Hansen (pp. 69–74) ask whether you are a collaborative leader, Abele (pp. 86–93) describes bringing minds together in community building, Adler et al., (pp. 95–101) give recommendations on how to build a collaborative enterprise, Fayard and Weeks suggest "creating workspaces that actually foster collaboration," (pp. 103–110), and Gavetti (pp. 118–125) promotes the power of associative thinking.

Another very interesting approach toward innovation is reported by Waytz and Mason in the 2013 July edition of the HBR. They write that Google gives company engineers 20% time, or, a day per week, to work on whatever they want to in order to facilitate innovation. Other companies that have followed suit to this approach are Maddock Douglas, Intuit, Bright-House, Twitter, and Atlassian. While time specifically for creativity is known to increase employees' sense of self-sufficiency, happiness, and motivation, their time is not really free, complain Waytz and Mason because they cannot escape the focus on the quantity of time they get (p. 105).

Innovation has also, of course, been an interest to neuroscience where new tools have made possible "insights into the biology of our minds and deepened our understanding of concepts crucial to managers, including: how to enable creative thinking" (Waytz and Mason, 2013: 104). What can neuroscience do for business? It can help business understand what's happening in the mind during important knowledge work such as creative thinking, decision making, multitasking, and pursuing rewards (p. 104).

The November 28 edition of *Time* magazine devoted a special double issue to the year's 50 best innovations (Grossman, 2011). More interesting than these inventions is Grossman's discussion of who the real inventors are – and Steve Jobs is not one of them! The fact that major business journals discuss innovation and creativity also points in the direction of another field of experts who have come up with a definition: creativity as the result of group efforts.

 In **Domain 4** Sawyer (2007) leads the charge in dismantling the idea of the lonely genius. It is eye-opening to follow his deconstruction of myths surrounding eminent individuals engaged in creating: Thomas

DOI: 10.1057/9781137531223.0007

Edison did not do it alone, and neither did Orville and Wilbur Wright, Sigmund Freud, or Einstein. As a matter of fact, Sawyer shows that "the most radical breakthroughs ... emerged from a collaborative web" (p. xi), through improvising innovation (chapter 2). Cain, similarly, writes that solitude is out of fashion, and lone geniuses are out (2012). They have been replaced with collaboration. Valsiner et al. phrase it this way: "Creativity is not a solitary process!" (2015: xx). A famous holdout to the idea that innovation is born in individuals is Steve Wozniak, cocreator of *Apple*, who in his memoir advises to work alone – because that worked for him (2006).

Sawyer is not alone in arguing the idea that creativity is born in groups. Martin (2011) and Galindo (2010) describe how the best creative thinking leading to innovation happens on companies' frontlines in groups. In the applied arts and design area, Oldach (1995) insists on managing process, team, and client for successful creative design. Hirshberg, founder and president of Nissan Design International (NDI), relates in his book on designing an organization around creativity (instead of the other way around) the history of NDI, and the enormous collaborative effort put out by his car design teams (1998). Gladwell agrees with Sawyer's arguments; while analyzing the US television show *Saturday Night Live* he observes that "We are inclined to think that genuine innovators are loners, that they do not need the social reinforcement that the rest of us crave. But that's not how it works, whether it's television comedy or, for that matter, the more exalted realms of art and politics and ideas" (2002b).

Csikszentmihalyi advises that among the factors contributing to innovative ideas are clear goals and feedback from other people so that the product or outcome is not just accepted by the environment, but is also deemed as having use (1999). One of the best examples of the power of group thinking is Thompson's research (2002) on open-source biology which represents the complete antithesis of corporatized research. Nobel Prize winner Alfred Gilman has organized a massive public brainstorm on the internet in order to rely on the collective wisdom of literally hundreds of biologists around the world, all working on the same problem. Neither Gilman nor anyone else involved in this project will be making any money from it. Thompson describes Gilman as wanting to tackle the big questions, open up all his and others' work, and let new ideas be bridged to new discoveries, because "we couldn't do all of this by ourselves. It's just too big. So we have to engage the entire community"

DOI: 10.1057/9781137531223.0007

(p. 2). What is interesting in this context is that brilliance, consistent with Sawyer's observations, is found in diverse groups thus decreasing corporate ownership of ideas and profits – something which, in the case of the Linux system development, has actually been called "un-American" by Microsoft operating systems chief Jim Alichin (Thompson, 2002: 2). Many scientists around the world are not only NOT interested in the money aspects of ideas, but they are also "more enthusiastic about working on open-source projects than anything locked up and corporate" (p. 3). Similar projects are posted on *Open IDEO*, the design firm's open innovation platform which invites people from around the world to submit their ideas not only for pesky product problems, but for social problems as well.

Collins does not explain innovative ideas as outcomes of groups, but rather as outcomes of networks, and states

> To see the development of ideas as the lengthened shadows of imposing personalities keeps us imprisoned in conventional reifications. We need to see through the personalities to dissolve them into the network of processes which have brought them to our attention as historical figures. (1998: 4)

Collins follows networks of ideas as they developed over centuries and explains the history of philosophy through examples such as German Idealism. "There is a social core: Fichte, Schelling, and Hegel, who once lived together in the same house" (p. 3), worked together, inspired each other, and then carried these ideas along to wherever they went for the rest of their lives. The network figures Collins generated to argue for this "social production of ideas" span the globe, uncovering groups and networks that made philosophy and creativity possible. Gladwell adds that Collins finds in all of known history "only three major thinkers who appeared on the scene by themselves: the first century Taoist metaphysician Wang Ch'ung, the 14th Century Zen mystic Bassur Tokusho, and the 14th Century Arabic philosopher Ibn Khaldun. Everyone else who mattered was a part of a movement, a school, a band of followers and disciples and mentors and rivals and friends who saw each other all the time and had long arguments over coffee and slept with one another's spouses" (2002b: 3).

Fischer agrees with Sawyer, Gladwell and Collins, by observing how

> The power of the unaided individual mind is highly overrated. Although society often thinks of creative individuals as working in isolation, creativity results in large part from interaction with other individuals. Much human

creativity is social, arising from activities that take place in a context in which interaction with other people and the artifacts that embody collective knowledge are essential. (CHI Conference, 2009)

One critic of Sawyer's proposal that creativity is the outcome of group efforts is Vincent Walsh who has doubted that creativity is a team sport (Skillicorn, 2014).

Missing in the preceding discussion on groups is one human trait frequently thought to be intimately connected to creativity, that is, intelligence.

In **Domain 5,** the theory on the correlation, if not causal relationship between, intelligence and creativity evolved from Spearman's (1927) supposition of a single unitary factor of intelligence called "g" (general intelligence) to a two-factor model of fluid and crystallized intelligence (Cattell, 1963), continuing to Sternberg's *Triarchic Theory of Successful Intelligence* (1985). Within this framework, creative intelligence represents the ability to respond effectively to novel situations, and successful intelligence represents an individual's ability to access all three factors in the solving of everyday problems. A similar description of the creation of multiple intelligences theory is provided by Feldman and Gardner (2003).

Gardner (1983) suggests that intelligence is composed of a series of independent abilities. Initially, he proposed a list of eight distinct intelligences (linguistic, logico-mathematical, musical, spatial, bodily-kinetic, naturalist, interpersonal, intrapersonal), and later added three more, that is, spiritual, existential, and naturalistic. However, Armstrong (1999) identifies only seven intelligences, and Brodbeck questions whether there are such things as general, intelligence-supporting social factors (2006: 5, translation mine) at all.

The close connection between creativity and intelligence has been discussed by Sternberg and Lubart (1999), and Feldman (with the collaboration of Gardner, in Sawyer et al., 2003) who calls it high level thinking. But the proposition that creativity is a sidekick of intelligence has been largely abandoned today, just like the proposition that creativity is the mad side of the Janus face, discussed next.

Domain 6 is broadly labeled "psychopathology," where the idea continues to live on that creativity is a born of insanity or at least a form of psychological impairment. There are numerous examples daily of this assumption in the public at large, and in the academic arena represented

DOI: 10.1057/9781137531223.0007

by Holm-Hadulla's (2010) analysis of the German poet Johann Wolfgang von Goethe's brilliance born of madness, and Andreasen's (2014) proposition that genius comes from psychological dysfunction.

Keynes, in a commentary on creativity and psychopathology, links the use of the "highest forms of human achievement,.. 'creativity'," to Aristotle's proposition of its relation to madness and states that "a link between creativity and a tendency to affective disorders has been firmly suggested" (1995: 138). Pathological personality characteristics were found to be present in geniuses also by Post (1994) who studied 291 world-famous men.

In an article on the puzzle of genius, Garber (2002) presents the arguments of Galton (1869) who equated genius to insanity and Bett (1952) who believed that geniuses were afflicted with insane infirmities and Lombroso (1895, 1911) who "asserted that genius was related both to moral degeneracy... and to certain physical characteristics," among which were beard deficiency, being short and being left-handed. Ellis (1904 [2009]), however, argues against the theory of genius as a form of insanity after investigating 975 eminent British men and 55 women. Yet, the myth continues as evidenced by the May edition of a German television magazine. Here, Riedemann "decodes the secrets" of those geniuses we are all familiar with, that is, Da Vinci, Einstein, von Goethe, but then concludes that everybody is a genius (2011, translation mine).

Creativity equated with either positive or negative deviance or dysfunction (e.g., Cusack, 1994; Eisenman, 1997; Keynes, 1995; Kusa, 2007) is frequently advocated: a few bright heads, a small circle of eminent people, equipped with unusual talent or insight, or, as in the case of Einstein, simply genius but a little odd. Freud's view of creativity (LaChapelle, 1983) as "only a small population of creative individuals in any given culture, and those individuals were usually found within the arts" (p. 132) is typical for that way in which creativity is perceived in modern Western society (see also Gardner's 1993 analysis of prominent geniuses). Much of what has been written describes eminents (Ludwig, 1995) or neurosis (LaChapelle, 1983: 152) and deals with questions of mental illness (see Post, 1994; Sutherland, 1995), or is seen as "the price for greatness" (Ludwig, 1995). Sutherland observes that "it remains an open question whether creative authors write to ease mental conflicts or whether they become eminent because these conflicts enrich their work" (1995: 548).

DOI: 10.1057/9781137531223.0007

The problem of genius, according to Garber, is not so much the yardstick we apply to measure whether people fit the term. The problem is that we have a deep-seated need in our society to glorify creative individuals, that is, "genius is an assessment or an accolade often retrospectively applied to an individual or an idea – not an identifiable essence" (2002: 65). We prefer the myth because we have an "occasionally desperate need to retain this ideal notion of the individual genius" (p. 66), and we do not separate the power of ideas from that of personality.

Psychiatrist and neuroscientist Nancy Andreasen (2014) insists that creativity is frequently accompanied by madness or mental illness. She found a high positive correlation between mental illness and highly creative people, and reports that the results of her research (based on 13 creative geniuses and 13 controls) confirm Galton's suggestion that genius seems to have a strong genetic component and seems to run in families. However, Bartlett (2014) has harshly criticized Andreasen's work, especially on methodological grounds. Becker (2008) similarly has criticized the psychopathological model from a sociological perspective.

Another approach is Eysenck's argument that psychoticism in personality, mostly based on physiological factors, could be directly related to creativity (Porzio, 2003; Eysenck, 1997). Here, it is theorized that "genetic and psychological traits of psychoticism and creativity are found to be greatly overlapping" (Porzio, 2003). The idea that madness and creativity are connected has become an established cultural and medical axiom in Western society, says Porzio, and our ideas about this connection are so deeply rooted that they are equivalent to the nocebo effect in clinical studies (p. 1). What could potentially change this perception of creativity would be education – but here we encounter yet more disagreement.

In **Domain 7**, Cropley argues (1999a, 1999b) that part of the task of liberal and humanistic education is to foster creativity by encouraging thinking in the classroom. Creativity comes from a variety of factors in his view, which are not included sufficiently in traditional classroom approaches to teaching creative thinking. Cropley relates that the original legislation emphasizing creativity in the classroom in the United States was the National Defense Act, that is, creativity became important culturally as a counterpoint to the Soviet Union winning the arms and space race. At the end of the 1990s, he argues, creativity is seen as important for competition and industry, and a vital concept for individuals' future because what they shall have learned in school may

DOI: 10.1057/9781137531223.0007

no longer be relevant by the time they hit job markets, and it would be creative thinking that gets them out of that conundrum.

Cropley also makes another point, "fostering creativity is not inconsistent with traditional school goals such as acquisition of knowledge and skills" (1999b: 631). But while teachers support the teaching of creativity in theory, they reward traditional behavioral traits in the classroom (obedience, respect, punctuality). This observation mirrors the results of the research provided in Chapter 4 of the present book. Employers and industry professionals say they are looking for creative people for their businesses, but they also say that the behavioral traits emphasized by Cropley are more important than creative minds. Creativity, to teachers, means troublesome students (Cropley, 1999a, 1999b, 2009) – and business owners and industry professionals would rather hire less creative, but reliable people than prima donnas who sparkle with creative ideas. Though Cropley's emphasis is on fostering creativity in the classroom, he rarely discusses the system of education which impedes the development and valuing of creativity – even in higher education (1997b).

Moffat (2010) describes creativity from a very different point of view: as a function of interpersonal relationships among faculty in a small college department. Creativity, here, is seen as facilitating collaboration, but there is little explanation of what would constitute creative outcomes. Tudor (2008) develops a pedagogy of creativity in order to understand higher-order capability development in design and arts education. She explains that creativity is "a catalyst for innovation, adaptability and survival in an increasingly unpredictable and rapidly changing world" (Abstract) and demands to actively teach for creativity. Where Tudor is falling short is in her focus on "those students with creative potential" (p. 7). Onground and MOOC (massive open online course) e-classes are reported to be increasingly teaching "Creativity Studies" since creativity is considered to be a higher-order skill, at the top of Bloom's Taxonomy of Learning objectives (Pappano, 2014). The educational system thus considers creativity a teachable and learnable skill.

Sir Ken Robinson (2010) of TED TALK fame is leading the camp of those critics who argue that creativity is systematically taught out of children as they grow up. He believes that children buzz with ideas and that something happens to them as they grow up (2010). The erratum here is the belief that children are born wonderfully creative, and then slowly but surely lose their "gifts," or that the educational system damages them for life. Propositions of creativity being normal or natural in children should be questioned. It is one thing to lament that we are losing our creative abilities as we grow older, and it is quite another to look at those so-called creative abilities (Robinson, 2001) and line them up with governments', companies', or organizations' needs to meet the demands of the 21st century. This recurring assertion that kids are highly, exclusively, and enviably so, creative by nature, and that adults rarely attain this state again after childhood, that is, "children transform boxes into spaceships, and sheets and furniture into elaborate forts by doing things differently" (Meyer, 2000: xiv) should be deconstructed because they do not need to earn a paycheck by making the spaceships fly, and their forts do not need to withstand an assault by enemies!

Shellenbarger (2010) blames rote learning and standardized testing for declining creativity scores among American children whereas Csikszentmihaly argues that "because creativity does not exist until it produces a change in culture, it cannot be observed or measured in children (unless children do change some domain of the culture, which hasn't happened yet, to my knowledge)" (in Sawyer et al., 2003: 223). Moran categorically declares that "(f)rom a Vygotskian perspective, children are not more creative than adults, because they have not mastered themselves or their skills" (pp. 223–224). Vygotsky proposes that "all human beings, *even small children* [emphasis added], are creative" (in Lindqvist, 2003) while Feldman believes that children "are not at all that creative because ... we romanticize childhood" (in Sawyer et al., 2003: 226). Glăveanu (2011a) investigated this question of children's natural creative predisposition from four different perspectives, that is, product, person, process, and press. He concludes that "recognising children's creativity is better than the alternative" (p. 129) because educators would want to value and foster creativity, a personal attribute that is highly valued in today's Western societies. Sawyer (in Sawyer et al., 2003: 240), on the contrary, states that the contributors to his book all agree that children are not creative.

In addition, argue Csikszentmihalyi and John-Steiner (in Sawyer et al., 2003), occasional bouts of creative thinking among children may be due to the fact that they have not yet internalized the rules of the domain. Sawyer links his students' belief that people could be more creative if they just discarded rules and constraints to "our culture's ingrained individualism: The free, unfettered individual is the greatest good, and the best society is one that just gets out of the way" (p. 227).

In a working paper of the German Federal Ministry of Education, Nickel (2011) discusses the European-wide effort to align its university programs with the Bologna Process across EU nations. Creativity at the university level has been investigated in Germany by Jahnke et al. (2011: 138–152). Contrary to Amabile who explains creativity as something defined by novelty and usefulness (1982, 1983a), they see creativity as meaning that has to be understood in context, that is, in the business world: an idea is creative when it leads to a product. It has a different meaning when it is applied to different areas/fields within universities (see, e.g., Anderson and Krathwohl's reorganization of Bloom's taxonomy [in Jahnke et al., 2011: 139]). Jahnke et al. find six facets of creativity in the BA and MA programs of three German universities, and the criteria for creativity are very different in the field of "Informatics" than in the field of "Mathematics" and the same goes for the field of "Languages/ Culture" and "Law/Economics/Social Sciences" as well (2011, translation mine). This finding mirrors the sociological theory developed in the next chapter that submits that what is considered creative is constructed in the domain or field in which it takes place.

While some experts believe that education needs to be changed from the ground up to facilitate creative thinking (Goldstein, 2010), others (Smith, 2008) suggest that "infusing a little creativity into our teaching.. makes us and our students better thinkers and learners" (p. 1). Smith's approach is more of a critique of traditional teaching methodology, and a call to break out of the obedient vein than a truly revolutionary call to creative arms. Here, concepts are mixed up in a martini shaker: a little bit of Sternberg and Lubart's six domains (1999) with a shot of Kohlberg's theory of moral development (1981) and a spritz of his ideas concoct his "pedagogy of creativity" (2008).

One empirical study to investigate whether student creative thinking can be improved was conducted by Karpova et al. who found that using creativity exercises in five courses did, indeed, lead to higher scores on a composite creativity index measured by the Torrance Test of Creative Thinking. This classic before-after experiment shows that the incorporation of creativity exercises helps to develop creative thinking, "a critical aspect of one's professional development" (2011: 1). The research team used several of the creativity exercises that are described in the Appendix to generate ideas, that is, von Oech, Michalko, and so on.

Both Cunliffe (2009) and Sawyer (2009) describe Gardner's ten-year rule, which is the idea of an educational journey that moves from unconscious incompetence of young children to conscious competence of adolescents into unconscious competence of adult experts. Creativity

DOI: 10.1057/9781137531223.0007

is seen as a process through time instead of a static trait of individuals or products (Sawyer et al., 2003). In a different vein from the ten-year rule, LaChapelle notes that "creative research extends beyond the research journals, and influences teachers' values and educational strategies" (1983: 131), and more importantly, "although the potential for creativity is present in everyone, its actualization depends upon a climate free from the pressures of conformity and harsh evaluation" (p. 132).

In contrast to many researchers who condemn schools and universities for their lack of creativity support, however, Csikszentmihalyi observes that "schools in general do a much better job to stimulate and nurture 'playful and innovative behaviors' in children" (in Sawyer et al., 2003: 223). Other pedagogical tools have been proposed by Tversky and Suwa who advocate the use of sketches in order to "amplify...imagination" (2009: 75), and Summers et al., who introduce design enabling tools to facilitate innovation – an exchange between academia and industry that is equivalent to a push and pull maneuver (2009: 195). Here, there are expressions and concepts that are new to creativity researchers: design enablers, concept trade-off exploration, reverse engineering – a completely different world. This approach is now detailed, alongside others that are either too small or too large to discuss individually.

Domain 8 introduces arguments from chaos theory, economic theory, the philosophy of creativity, design thinking for social innovations, social creativity (which is a different concept than that of Domain 5), and biomimickry design. **Chaos theory** argues that beliefs change because science changes in unforeseen ways, and monolithic understandings are shaken in their foundations because of unexpected insights (Küppers, 1993: 28, translation mine).Scriba (1993) explains how creativity emerges from systems that are non-calculable, self-organizing, and deterministic. What we take for granted may just need a little bit of creative thinking, and our reality is changed. Thus, the answer to the question by Mandelbrot "how long is the coast of Great Britain?" is that it depends on the measuring tape – the finer the tape, the closer to infinity the length (p. 55, translation mine). Sommer (1993: 64–70) suggests that creativity is the unplanned, and that the playful is a central element of becoming (e.g., many cultures' and religions' dances and games that are age-old but often no longer understood in their origins) (translation mine).

Chaos, or nonlinear dynamical systems theory, is explained by Schuldberg (1999) as "change with time" (p. 260), rejecting cross-sectional and short-term relationships between variables. Similarly, ideas according to which complex societal systems are planned are considered naive by German sociologist Luhman (Wehowsky, 1993) who says that social systems organize themselves, and are hard – if not impossible – to influence and direct. Such chaotic systems become immune to planned changes and survive through autopoiesis (i.e., self-organization) by reverse coupling. Social systems are thus creative, unpredictable, and always in danger of destruction if their environments do not uphold them (Wehowsky, 1993: 158, translation mine).

Economic theory is applied to creativity with an emphasis on monetary rewards from creative endeavors and innovations. In contemporary meanings of economics, the ideal of a community of craftsmen "to whom the ancient appellation *demioergoi* (i.e., public producers) can be applied" (Sennett, 2008) has long been lost in capitalist societies, including the capacity to exercise creative thinking through applying skill (Mills, 1951). But creativity also embodies gigantic financial potential as Howkins has pointed out (2002). He estimates that the creative economy generates $ 2.2 trillion a year globally.

An intriguing link of law and economics of creativity in the workplace is discussed by Orbach of Harvard Law School in 2002. Here is a completely new spin to the question of creativity, that is, who owns the rights to creative products, employers or employees? He argues that "the distinctive properties of creative workers and the characteristics of their employment do not justify workers' ownership" (2002: 1) – a significant monkey wrench into Florida's (2002) vision of happy workers who enjoy the fruits of their creative labor. Lubart and Runco (1999), in an extension of the economic argument, propose an interesting marriage of micro-, and macroeconomics of creativity, their so-called investment theory of creativity –the principle of buying low and selling high.

Galenson, of the University of Chicago's National Bureau of Economic Research (2009), repeats assertions that creativity is "largely the domain of extraordinary individuals or small groups" (p. 1) and results in the "vast productivity of these exceptional individuals "(p. 2). He also argues that "innovation is a leading source of improving standards of living" for artists, which enables enormous economic benefits for societies (2004a, 2004b, 2006). Joseph Schumpeter's creative destruction model of innovation spurts that destroy existing worlds and bring new ones was considered hot in Washington DC in the early years of the new millennium (Rose, 2002), also an outgrowth of economic theories.

DOI: 10.1057/9781137531223.0007

So far, I have not mentioned the most important field that has influenced all others: **the philosophy of creativity**. Here we encounter not only old Greeks and assumptions of a God who hands out creative genius, but also theories that underpin social science questions such as, is human nature creative, is creativity innate in humans, or does it evolve from environments? The *Conference on the Philosophy of Creativity* adds the following questions: What is creativity? How does it happen? How is it that creativity is manifest in discovery as well as invention, in science as well as art? In what ways might an audience participate in creating a work of art? What role does creativity play in the construction of the self? (Barnard College, 2010).

The philosophy of creativity is, for Fox (2004), a question of divinity. The word comes from theology and initially described the "creator." This term was transferred, during the 17th Century to the eminent human, henceforth called the "genius" (p. 3). The term creativity does not even appear in the German encyclopedia of 1894 (Reck, 2008). It was subsequently the process of democratization in society which provided an extension of the concept to all humans, signaling the end of the age of genius. For this argument, see also Glăveanu's explanation of "He, I, and We paradigms" (2010, p. 148).

Silver et al. (undated) outline philosophies of creativity and begin with Genesis 1, moving on to Herder, Marx, Schopenhauer, Nietzsche, Simmel, Weber, Durkheim, James, Dewey, Marcuse, Joas, Parsons, Mead, Jacob, and Bellah... to mention just a few. Their thesis concerns creative cities with a concentration on quantitative evaluation of, among other variables, bohemia and the arts. Noteworthy is their handling of Max Weber's phrase "every man a monk" which they change to "every man a musician" and tie to the generation of new ideas and styles. Also intriguing is their idea of an "iron cage of creativity," that is, "innovate or die? Bohemia or Bust?" (undated).

An action theory approach to the question of the role of creativity and pragmatism is submitted by Gimmler (2006) who invited Hans Joas and Richard Sennett to a discussion on the importance of creativity in the social sciences. Joas and Sennett point to the new contemporary form of capitalism which "threatens not only social integration and the integrity of individual life courses but in the end creativity as such" (p. 5). Joas ties the idea of creativity to the idea of self-realization, and to the Marxian ideal of realizing oneself through work, where production becomes "creativity in the realm of material objects," and people helping each

DOI: 10.1057/9781137531223.0007

other (in the tradition of Herder) to exercise creativity in conflict resolutions through role taking (p. 8). Sennet responds that "Creativity isn't a state. The creative process is always a process of being able to objectify" (p. 9). The notion that creativity is exclusively reserved for artists is rejected by both thinkers, and Sennett proposes that "you are not just creative as a human being or one being is more creative than the other, but you are creative within particular situations... The challenge is to be creative under certain conditions" (p. 11).

Danish philosopher Klausen (2010) adds a new wrinkle to the discussion by insisting that it is the product, not the person or the process, that should be seen as creative. Especially noteworthy is his observation that "there is a tendency to assimilate the definition of the entity under study to those properties that happen to be most conveniently measurable" (p. 348). He is highly critical of a notion of creativity that seems to be limited to a Western, Anglo-Saxon interpretation which includes the idea that in order to be considered creative, something has to be "necessarily successful" (p. 349). Moreover, Klausen mentions one issue that is important in the discussion of the next chapter, that is, "the definition makes creativity dependent on *social acceptance*" (p. 349, Italics by Klausen).

A very different approach to viewing creativity is furnished by Brown and Wyatt's **Design Thinking for Social Innovation**. Here, design tools are used to tackle health care or clean water supply problems (2007). Design thinking is "a new approach to creating solutions" (p. 32), engineering entire systems for delivery of products and services, and for the needs of consumers. It originates in IDEO (Kelley, 2001, 2005; Kelley and Kelley, 2013), a firm that designs not only products but also consumer experiences, and "taps into capacities we all have but that are overlooked by more conventional problem-solving practices" (Brown and Wyatt, 2007: 33).

IDEO's focus has, in Europe, shifted from pure product design to service design and designing engineering services for both nongovernmental organizations (NGOs) and governments (Schumpeter, 2013). There are three important elements: (1) lots of different eyes – people from different backgrounds in a team; (2) looking at issues from a customer's point of view while focusing on the outliers (people with more elaborate problems); and (3) everything is tangible, so mock-ups are constantly being built for every product, and then tested in the "wild" (Schumpeter, 2013). Brown, the CEO of IDEO, describes in his book on design thinking (2009) how creativity lurks in the most obvious, but often overlooked

DOI: 10.1057/9781137531223.0007

locations, for example, hospital frontline staff presenting ideas to develop changes in their organization. IDEO's human-centered approach drives the creative thinking that leads to innovation and to economic growth.

David Kelley says that anybody can be creative, but has to learn how. He is cofounder of IDEO and the founder of the Stanford University's Hasso Plattner Institute of Design ("the d.school") where he tasks groups of students to come up with solutions to global problems through learning by doing, designing prototypes through speed and quantity so that failure is a necessity on the way to success, learning through collaboration across disciplines, and a democratic learning process where everyone has an equal voice (Kelley and Kelley, 2013; Geer, 2011b). The results/innovations from the d.school are impressive, as are its birthing of several companies along the way, and efforts to teach K-12 teachers how to employ its techniques with their students (Geer, 2011a, 2011b). Sawyer (2014), for example, recommends that creativity researchers take a closer look at this idea of design thinking where "creators turn their ideas into physical reality early and often, through prototyping and iterative design" (p. xiv). The Stanford Design Program (undated) advertises itself as a place that develops new transdisciplinary methodologies in order to tackle such problems as "energy, widespread behavior change, and complex business changes" (http://designprogram.stanford.edu). The d.school's design thinking process is a series of steps (understand, observe, define, ideate, prototype, test) which loop forward and backward and point to all directions and earlier and later steps. For more information, visit the Stanford Social Innovation Review at www.ssireview.org/articles/entry/ design_thinking_for_ social_ innovation/. A free guide to innovation for social enterprises and NGOs is available at the www.ideo.com/work/human-dcentered-design-toolkit/ website.

A very different and unusual approach to design, innovation, and problem solving is **biomimickry**, which was suggested in the late 1990s. According to one of its leaders, Janine Benyus, "innovation is inspired by nature" (designboom, undated) because nature has already found solutions for many human problems. This approach is especially useful for designers whose job it is to solve technical problems. Benyus biomimickry guild which she founded in 1998 is a consulting firm, and in 2008, established an alliance with architectural corporation, HOK. The biomimickry community created the *design spiral* specifically for designers to adhere to nature's inspiration for their work (i.e., integrating form, process, and ecosystem). Some of the outcomes of this

DOI: 10.1057/9781137531223.0007

design approach are the shinkansen bullet train, Mercedes-Benz bionic concept vehicle, an entropy carpet, whale power wind turbines, lotus effect textiles, paint and glass surfaces that can clean themselves, fabrics which exhibit shimmering colors without having color pigments, fibers made from spider silk that are tougher than nylon or steel, dry adhesives which are based on the microstructure of the gecko's foot, biological springs that imitate jellyfish stings, telephone and internet lines that are structured like venus flower baskets resembling mineral basketworks, and air conditioning systems that are based on the habitats of African termites (designboom, undated; Forbes, 2005). Another application, albeit on a much grander scale, are the world's first cities, Lavasa and Mugaon in India, inspired by nature (www.lavasa.com; www.hok.com/about/sustainability/lavasa-hill-station-master-plan; www.biomimicry-guild.com; www.hok.com; HOK, undated). One of the earliest and best-known examples of biomimickry is George de Mestral's invention of Velcro (see www.designboom.com). Out for a walk with his dog, he tried to remove burr seed sacs that had attached themselves to his dog's coat, and the idea for Velcro was born!

Epstein (2010), a highly regarded designer, delivers recommendations for the corporate creatives which includes the designers who work in teams in corporations and have to learn to be managers as well as people who know how to cut through the red tape. Designers, to Epstein, are different animals who cannot be pressed into existing bureaucratic pegholes, and they are different because they are designers! – so that "as a creative, you really are different from your peers in the corporate world" (p. 3). A very different creativity is proposed by British designer, computer programmer, and creative digital art director Daniel Brown who combines play and creativity in his company Play-Create Ltd. (for his design work, see http://danielbrowns.com). Selected as one of Internet Business Magazine's top ten internet designers as well as named on Creative Review's list of "Stars of the New Millennium," Brown was injured in a swimming accident, and is now disabled, unable to move either legs or fingers. Yet, he continues to produce amazing designs and artwork.

Fischer (2011) argues for **social creativity** in order to harness the power of cultures of participation. This way of defining creativity sees pressing problems in our world that need solving through collaboration, which is made possible through technology facilitated by meta designers. The assumption is that cultures of participation offer the chance to cope with problems because technologies "engage audiences, enhance

DOI: 10.1057/9781137531223.0007

creativity, share information, and foster collaboration among...active contributors and designers" (p. 1). What is presupposed in Fischer's vision of meta design environments are knowledgeable participants. The battle cry emerging from this perspective is: MAKE ALL THE VOICES HEARD!!

At the 2009 CHI conference, panelists from diverse intellectual backgrounds and national and industry cultures discussed the "creative challenges and opportunities in social computing." Social computing and theories of creativity that recognize the social construction of creativity were combined. One interesting question for the panels at the 2009 CHI conference was whether seeds for a more creative society can be sown by educating students in creative mindsets. This assumption that creativity can be taught is the basis for the discussions in the next domain.

Domain 9 – **commercial consulting.** A commercial industry of consulting has sprung up around the perceived need to foster creativity and innovation in US businesses (Jana, 2008). One bizarre example includes trying out innovative coaching by advisors who recite ancient Indian texts in front of employees in order to foster the development of new products (Jana, 2008) There is even mention of the development of "innovation economics" (Mandel, 2008), that is, the widespread belief of US economists and business leaders that "innovation is the best – and maybe only – way the U.S. can get out of its economic hole" (p. 52). But if we are to create our way out of economic recession, we need people to teach us how to be creative!

Hundreds of gurus and approaches have come and gone. Some models have been incredibly successful such as the Oz Group at the DuPont Corporation (Tanner, 1997; DuPont Employees, 1990), which saved the company millions of Dollars. When Tanner retired, however, the Oz Group fell apart, and creativity as a corporate goal took a backseat (2010, personal e-mail exchange with Dr. Tanner). One of the most popular teachings of creativity was that of Edward De Bono (1985) on whose ideas the Oz Group at DuPont had been based. He invented the different colored thinking hats, but again, this approach has faded away since De Bono retired and sold the company.

It is important to mention here as an example for corporate creativity training, the Center for Creative Leadership (ccl@creativeleadership. com), which describes itself as "a top-ranked, global provider of executive education that accelerates strategy and business results by unlocking the leadership potential of individuals and organizations." With a focus

DOI: 10.1057/9781137531223.0007

exclusively on leadership education and research, CCL helps clients worldwide to cultivate creative leadership. Ranked among the world's top ten providers of executive education by *Bloomberg Business Week* and the *Financial Times*, CCL is headquartered in Greensboro, NC, with locations around the world, supported by more than 500 faculty and staff.

Today, consulting firms teach a wide variety of creative approaches, just with different tools. The Appendix gives an idea on how wide this how-to industry has spread. As may be (and maybe even painfully) obvious from the differences in approach, there is a lot of discussion of, and making money with, the concept of creativity, but little empiricism, and certainly no agreement on its meaning. When looking for academic substance, and properly built models, as well as tested theories, we have to turn our attention to the field of psychology where the empirical study of creativity officially began in 1950.

Domain 10 – psychology. This section must begin with Guilford's 1950 address to the American Psychological Association which laid the groundwork for the following 65 years of research in the field of Psychology. He asked the first questions about the creative personality, the correlation between education and creative productiveness, about how the creative promise in children and young people could be discovered – and he challenged the association to come up with appropriate testing procedures. Interestingly, he questioned the belief of genius as intelligence or IQ, and linked creativity to learning. But essentially, his focus was on the person, and he conceded that "creative acts can... be expected, no matter how feeble or how infrequent, of almost all individuals" (1950: 446). For a detailed history of creativity in Psychology, see Albert and Runco (1999) and Mayer (1999).

Traditionally, psychologists have seen creativity as an innate phenomenon which represents "a quality of a person or a product" (Glăveanu and Gillespie, 2015: 2). The view of creative people, whether in the arts or sciences, was often that of the composer Mozart, painter Da Vinci, or physicist Einstein in isolation, producing phenomenal ideas. This was considered an internal process, as creativity pouring out of the genius personality. It has been, thus, "the most basic unit of creativity ... as many assume, a particular personality trait, thinking style, or cognitive mechanism, or a neurological structure?" (p. 3).

Economist Galenson (2006) echoes this traditional conception of creativity and links the importance of the creator to the wide spreading of his/her innovation (p. 30). Psychologist of science Feist investigated

DOI: 10.1057/9781137531223.0007

questions related to creativity such as why there "are some people able to solve apparently intractable problems with elegant, original and useful solutions?" and "why are some individuals consistently able to come up with creative solutions to scientific problems?" (Ross, 2005).

One group of psychologists emphasizes environmental variables which are thought to support or depress the development of creativity. Thus, Richman states that "[t]he development of creativity probably depends upon a nurturant and facilitating environment in the family, in the interpersonal network, and in society. Mentors, models and a special companion or companions often play an essential role" (1997: 449) but Vygotsky declares that higher mental capacities are based in culture, not biological functions (in Sawyer et al., 2003). Csikszentmihalyi insists that "the phenomenon of creativity is as much a cultural and social, as it is a psychological event" (in Sternberg, 1999: 313) and criticizes that "[t]he enduring belief that great creativity is developed largely alone, without assistance from teachers, mentors, peers and intimate groups is largely a myth" (in Feldman, 1999).

Several psychological approaches to creativity do not fit easily into established schools or orientations. Kusa (2007) focuses entirely on the creator and the intrapersonal, and Gudmund Smith (2008) emphatically declares "I wholly agree with Runco...that emphasis on social factors is beside the point, a way to avoid the crucial questions in creativity research" (p. 383). That way of describing the concept, one which takes a macrosociological look at an explanation for creativity, is discussed in the next chapter.

DOI: 10.1057/9781137531223.0007

3
A Sociological Model of Creativity

Abstract: *This chapter recounts the prevalence as well as the lack of discussion of creativity in the Sociology domain. Rarely discussed by American sociologists, the concept has been theorized in German Sociology, especially in action theory. The "Sociological Imagination," a lens through which to critically assess creativity, is introduced in this chapter, and the arguments of social constructionism are presented. The need to integrate issues of culture is briefly outlined, and the preeminence of American methodologies is questioned. The first macrosociological model of creativity in the literature is mapped out and its various stages are explained. Finally, this chapter presents arguments against social constructionism.*

Reuter, Monika E. *Creativity – A Sociological Approach.* Basingstoke: Palgrave Macmillan, 2015. DOI: 10.1057/9781137531223.0008.

DOI: 10.1057/9781137531223.0008

Sociologists (except for discussing art, e.g., Becker, 1974, 1982; Alexander, 2003) have taken a radically different approach to the interpretation of creativity, that is, almost none! They use the concept, but do not define it. A recent article published in the journal *Social Forces* is an excellent example for the cavalier handling of the concept: individuals' work values are described as both intrinsically and extrinsically oriented, where people want to have the kind of jobs that Florida (2002) foresaw for our future, with high pay, security, and the ability to express themselves creatively (Kirkpatrick and Mortimer, 2011). What, however, do Kirkpatrick and Mortimer mean by 'creative expression'? They do not explain.

Kurt and Göttlich (2012) have edited one of the only few German sociological publications on creativity and lament that it is as remarkable as it is weird that Sociology has not yet systematically investigated questions of creativity except for symbolic interactionist approaches of action theory (translation mine). German sociologists Joas (1996) and Reckwitz (2012) write about creativity, but from a very different angle than what is described in the present book. Several other sociologists have dealt with creativity in a tangential way, that is, Pettinger (undated) explores creativity with an emphasis on economic success. Tepper (2003) mentions creative process, inventions, and entrepreneurship in his Sociology SOC214 class syllabus at Princeton. He investigates the social context for innovation and creativity, which means the social relationships and networks that surround creative works, gate keeping, innovation and new technologies as well as institutional changes.

Göttlich and Kurt's book discusses creativity predominantly from the point of view of action theory. Schäfer, one of the contributors, says that ever since Joas, the concept of pragmatism, that is, radical anticartesian philosophy has been at the center of German sociological analyses of creative actions (2012, translation mine).

Every facet of human social life, from race to sexuality, has been investigated by Sociology. Yet there has been no formal sociological theory of creativity although eminent sociologist George Ritzer declares, "I'd like to see a society in which people are free to be creative, rather than having their creativity constrained or eliminated" by the process of McDonaldization (www.georgeritzer.com). Some psychological arguments overlap with sociological insights so that, for example, the concept of *Zeitgeist* is seen as influencing and perhaps even determining creativity (Simonton, 1999b). That would imply that the taste du jour/week/month/year shapes what creativity is.

DOI: 10.1057/9781137531223.0008

Within Sociology, discussions of art have entailed the use of the concept where one sociologist is preoccupied with the production and consumption of culture (Tanner, 2003) while another (Pettinger, undated) says that activities defined as creative, and what creativity entails, are socially defined processes. Alexander (2003) proposes that there is no art unless there are people willing to pay for it, and Becker (1982) finds that art worlds cannot even exist unless there are many other people aiding the artist. Bourdieu (1979) takes a different point of view and sees as the basis for creativity in art not quality, but snobbism and power relationships. He asks who has the power to declare cultural artifacts as creative.

Sociology is the ideal domain to investigate creativity. The *Sociological Perspective* is a way of thinking beyond one's blinders, taking a wider – *much, much wider!* – look around one's society, one's belief systems, one's values, one's knowledge than traditional individualistic interpretations take. Originally coined by C. Wright Mills (1959) and elaborated upon by Giddens (1982), having a *Sociological Imagination* enables the connection of one's biography to the history of the society in which one lives; it encourages viewing individuals as both outcomes as well as architects of their social world; it requires a capacity to see one's personal problems as embedded within larger social issues – unemployment, for example, as a personal hardship but also as a consequence of economic forces beyond the influence of individuals. To lose one's job due to globalization often results in the loss not just of income, but also of health insurance and other benefits. Sociologists of Work and Occupations would also argue that the loss of a job entails the loss of one's master status, and often, friends. Moreover, job loss is connected to decisions made by the corporation one has worked for, the bonus which the CEO will get at the end of the year because s/he saved a lot of money by outsourcing jobs, and the relocation of those jobs to India where they will provide an opportunity for a lower-caste member to join a newly forming middle class (see Morgan Spurlock's episode 'Outsourcing' in his 2009 *30 Days* television series).

Unemployment is so much more than just an individual's experience. It also describes a social problem as more and more people lose jobs and as unemployment statistics do not adequately describe the problem. The long-term unemployed, for example, are no longer counted in official US Department of Labor Statistics since they are no longer eligible for benefits. From a very different point of view, unemployment can, in

DOI: 10.1057/9781137531223.0008

addition, be seen as both a cause and a consequence of stock market crashes – even if those stock market problems originate somewhere else in the world, and then "swap over" to Europe or the United States, literally overnight.

A Sociological Imagination makes it possible to take off one's blinders, and locate oneself in a much larger environment than previously experienced. Things never thought of before as influencing people's lives become real: values, beliefs, norms, race, gender, age, inequality, actors who define our fate but whom we will never meet such as the president of the United States who makes a decision to go to war, or a board of directors deciding to move its manufacturing plant and the mid-level management team half-way across the world. All of these things are, in turn, connected to a specific time and culture, especially what that time and culture means to societies in the Western world as opposed to those in Africa.

Giddens (1982) views Sociology as critique, that is, a "three-fold exercise of the Sociological Imagination … (requires) … an historical, an anthropological, and a critical sensitivity" (p. 13). Awareness of history means tracing of meaning. For Giddens that is an understanding of the Industrial Revolution. For the purpose of a sociological theory that describes the social construction of creativity, it is understanding that institutions (schools, professional organizations, associations) play a part in the formation of creativity. Dispensing with ethnocentrism means shaking off the belief, implicit or explicit, that the modes of life which have developed in the Western world are somehow superior to those of other cultures (p. 19). We have a tendency to take our own culture as a measure to judge all others. Critical thinking refers, for Giddens (1982), to a capacity to critique existing forms of society. Just because we live in this one (or that one, for that matter) does not mean it is the best one.

A personal story can illustrate this experience of the Sociological Imagination. Even though I have spent the majority of my life outside of Germany, the country where I was born and still hold citizenship, and even though being German is much less important to me than it is to other people, I become keenly aware of being German when Americans ask me where I am from. At this point, I could possibly say that I am from South Florida, but that would not be entirely true. In every conversation I have had about where I am from, it is inevitable that my country's history comes up as a topic. I was born years after the end of World War II but

DOI: 10.1057/9781137531223.0008

am deeply aware of the political and philosophical questions connected to it, as well as holocausts that are happening around the world right now. No matter how long I will live, and how many more years I live in the United States, I will always be a German to others – whether I want to or not, and even if I took American citizenship! The history of the country has shaped, and is attached to, my biography – and to that of my daughter who was born in 1991. When other high school students found out that she had been born in Germany, and that her mother was German, her nickname in her last year at high school was "Little Nazi." A Sociological Imagination permits people to see connections and to understand how they, and everybody around them, engage in shaping our world, our history, our communal experiences, and our personal lives.

A Sociological Imagination also enables people to think beyond their own cultural experiences and appreciate other ways of life. Not better, not worse than our own. Just different. A very poignant and striking example of a nonethnocentric and critical view that would be consistent with Giddens' threefold sociological imagination is the opening scene of the first episode of the HBO television show *The Newsroom* (www.youtube. com). There is hardly a better way to exercise historical understanding, anthropological sensitivity, and critical evaluation than is depicted by television anchor Will's response to a naive student's question of why America is the greatest country in the world.

Creativity as social construction

For mankind, what we need to know, we must be taught (Kirton, 2010)

After reviewing creativity from ten very different domains in the previous chapter, a theory of creativity based on the premises of social construction is now presented. In order to support this thesis, the meaning of the term "social construction" needs to be explored. Helpful in this endeavor is psychologist Gergen's (2010: 58) advice that "social constructivism invites the appreciation of multiple perspectives" and that it initiates a form of discourse instead of seeking to be a final word (p. 166).

Gergen's argument for constructivism is as follows: in *The Republic*, Plato (1992) relates the allegory of the cave, that is, the effects of education, and the question of what reality is. Gergen uses the same line of reasoning by employing the example of one-year-old Julie who sees the same things as adults do when they take her for a walk. The meanings of their surroundings, however, would be interpreted quite differently by Julie than by adults (2010: 3). Important in Gergen's proposal of social construction from a psychological point of view is his insight of Communicamus, ergo sum (we communicate, therefore I am) (160). Who I am is constructed out of interactions with others so that people create self-definition "largely within conversations" (p. 69), an argument that resembles sociologist Charles Horton Cooley's theory of *the looking glass self (looking glass* was the word for "mirror" in 19th-century America). According to Cooley, we construct ourselves depending on what we believe other people believe about us (Benokraitis, 2012: 68) while Gergen observes that "our actions are based not on the way the world is, but on the meaning it has for ... individual(s)" (p. 26).

Several other compelling examples of how social construction works are furnished by an anthropologist, a psychological anthropologist, and a sociologist. Everett's brilliant and radical refutation of Chomsky's theory of language (2012) is a gripping example of social construction, as is his fascinating description of life among the Pirahã tribe in the Amazon rainforest for over 30 years (2008). Luhrmann's (2012) spellbinding research on how evangelical Christians talk to God, and how he talks back to them, is equally an investigation into a social construction of reality, as is Torlina's (2011) riveting look at Marx's assumptions of aliena-tion as an inevitable by-product of blue-collar work. All of these works eradicate long-held and deep-seated beliefs about what language is, how Evangelical churches direct believers in their conversations with God, and that stone masons are not necessarily alienated. All of these works describe how social construction works.

Constructionists such as Gergen (2010) would argue that what crea-tivity means is constantly changing. In addition, following German journalist Neffe (2008: 208), it makes sense that "nobody is born with the capacity to build a canoe" (translation mine). Neffe's observation suggests that creativity is not inborn, but constructed and learned.

Creativity should be seen as constructed within cultural meaning systems. If you live in the Amazon rainforest like anthropologist Everett (2008), you have to learn how to build a canoe because it is vital to your and your tribe's survival. If you live in France, Great Britain, or the United States, your survival does not depend on having learned how to build a canoe, but how to navigate technology. Eminent social-psychologist Csikszentmihalyi emphasizes this importance of environment by

DOI: 10.1057/9781137531223.0008

declaring that "creativity is as much a cultural and social as it is a psychological event" (1999: 313). We need to bring the issue of culture into the discussion of the social construction of creativity – not just the culture of the Amazon rainforest or the culture of China or Poland, but also the cultures of fields and domains. This point will be revisited later in this chapter. First, however, the original conception of *social construction* within Sociology needs to be briefly addressed.

Berger and Luckmann (1967) are the sociologists who coined the term *social construction of reality*. They propose that knowledge is built from, and maintained through, social interaction. It then becomes an objective reality. It is important to point out that one of the biggest critics of constructionism is Thomas Luckmann himself who stated in an interview, "I have never considered myself a constructionist" (2010, translation mine). He does, however, explain what he considers "construction," by saying, "In a Marxist sense: humans make the human world. That is Marx, pure Marx" (2010: 362, translation mine). He also explains typical models of human experiences constructed in long historical chains of especially communicative actions, and which then represent for all humans the societal-historical *a priori* of their reality (Luckmann, 2003, translation mine). He claims that "different societies form different types of personal identity. Actions are regulated by specialized institutions in concrete domains. Action orientation and norms of behavior are often not easily, or not at all, transferrable from one domain to another" (pp. 391–392, translation mine).

In addition, Luckmann (2008) proposes that "once a world view is grounded in a society, it becomes a forced system of interpretations. This is how a world view achieves the inevitability of a subjective knowledge category, and the objectivity of a cultural norm which is henceforth shared by every normal human" (p. 37, translation mine). For Luckmann, historical reality emerges from societal action, which, in turn, emerges from conscious action (p. 34, translation mine). Furthermore, he explains (2004: 27) that "eversince Thukidides, via Vico and Marx, the opinion has been that human realities are historical realities which emerge and are supported in social action" (translation mine). He proposes that "the meaning of individual action, essentially subjective, is mostly derived from social stocks of knowledge. These, of course, do not arise by themselves. They are built up in communicative social interaction," and "the human social world is already mainly constructed in communicative interaction," where "reconstructions feed the collective memory of families, social groups and classes, institutions and entire societies" (2012).

So, how can Luckmann's theory of reality as a consequence of social interactions and actions be interpreted? Consistent with Marx, we construct our worlds, and our worlds then construct us. Creativity does not exist in and of itself; it comes into being because it is given meaning by a cultural context, and that meaning then changes within the culture. One cannot meet Ms. Creativity, shake her hand, or talk with her. She does not exist. So, how does creativity come to be real? Just like crime comes to be real as we define what is criminal, Gergen (2010) argues, we also define what is mental illness. Neither one, he says, exist in nature. Everyday lives have meaning only because of everyday interactions. For many sociologists, *everything is socially constructed* – race, gender, values, beliefs, norms, including even sexuality (Seidman, 2010) or time (Lemonick, 1999; Boslough, 1990).

Berger and Luckmann's (1967: 3) theory suggests that the question should be asked how a definition of creativity is taken for granted in one society, but not in another. The process by which creativity comes to be socially established as reality pertains to specific social contexts (p. 3). For the arguments proposed in the present book, Marx is correct that "man's consciousness is determined by his social being" (Berger and Luckmann, 1967: 6) so that social being is shaped in a school, a fashion boutique, a design studio, a classroom – all social contexts where creativity means something different. Scheler (in Berger and Luckmann, 1967: 8) analyzes the manner in which any human knowledge is ordered by society, positing knowledge as an "a priori to individual experience," that is, meaning. Mannheim's proposition that there is no human thinking which is "immune to the ideologizing influence of its social context" (p. 9) means that knowledge must always be knowledge from a certain position (p. 10).

Similar to Berger and Luckmann, Sales et al., Stehr, Hage, Urry, Calhoun, Fuller, Breton, and Hollingsworth (all in Sales and Fournier, 2007; see also Sales et al., 2007: 4) propose that the source and result of social change in contemporary society can be found in knowledge, communication, networks, and creativity. What counts today, Sales et al. (2007) insist, is creativity and innovation because they are both tied to socioeconomic development (p. 6). Knowledge societies, as Stehr calls them, are those where knowledge strengthens creativity as well as where knowledge production demands creativity (p. 6). Sales et al. cite

DOI: 10.1057/9781137531223.0008

sociologist Joas' assertion that every human action is potentially creative (p. 14). Yet, as Collins points out in Sales and Fournier (2007), all knowledge is produced within networks – and is hence socially constructed. Hollingsworth investigates this "issue of society's capacity to create creativity" (Sales et al., 2007: 18; Reuter, 2011b).

Sales and Fournier and their coauthors mirror Bijker et al.'s (1987), Pinch and Bijker's (1984), and Winner's (1993) analyses of the social construction of technological systems (SCOT). Social reality and phenomena such as creativity are constructed, institutionalized, and handed down to new generations within fields as traditions until they are reconstructed, newly institutionalized, and handed down again. Latour makes a crucial observation talking about the innovation of the Diesel engine: Rudolf Christian Karl Diesel had not just an idea for an engine, but also how his engine would impact the world economically and socially, and he even went as far as to design the type of society that would be the best fit for his invention (Latour, 1987: 107).

Just as colors do not exist independently, that is, they come alive only as humans perceive light waves that hit their retinas, creativity has meaning only within a social context. There is no such thing as color. There is no such thing as creativity. One does not learn creativity, but one learns how to think more creatively in various fields. Circles of fashion designers declare what is creative (see Vangkilde, in this chapter), employers and industry professionals have very firm ideas about the meaning of creativity (see the research in Chapter 4), and all of those have fundamentally different ideas of what is creative in their fields than painters or sculptors do. Moreover, judgments of taste, as Bourdieu (1979) has pointed out, are a function of social position.

Berger and Luckmann say that "the man in the street does not ordinarily trouble himself about what is 'real' to him.. he takes his 'reality' and his 'knowledge' for granted" (1967: 2). In general, the public takes things that surround its culture for granted, technological things just as well as experiences, definitions or belief systems. People rarely question – be it globalization or what creativity is. These are issues that are politically and ideologically shaped by experts. Yet, if one possesses a Sociological Imagination, one is able to consider the idea that even identities are socially constructed and negotiated (Abercrombie, 2004: 8–9). We have no true selves in this view, but we are constructed/conditioned/socialized early on from birth, and then construct ourselves continuously, embedded in, and a product of, the cultures around us. This is a difficult

DOI: 10.1057/9781137531223.0008

idea to wrap one's mind around in Western societies which emphasize, especially in the United States, deeply ingrained beliefs about rugged individualism, unique personality, and freedom to be who one wants to be.

The vast differences in definitions concerning creativity come from a constructed acceptance of reality so that a graphic designer understands what creativity is in her field, just as a web designer does – and these realities differ substantially. Creatives and the circles around them are continuously engaged in the process of teaching and constructing what is in or out, for example, fashion designers moving from mini to maxi to midi, interior designers moving from formica countertops to granite. Creativity thus becomes a function of human activity and the social relations that come from this activity, that is, humans make creativity, creativity does not make humans. Stated differently by Russian psychologist Gaidenko,

> Creativity always takes place under specific social and historical conditions, which profoundly influence it. Creativity is closely linked with the environment and with previously created cultural forms, whose complex network includes the agent of the creativity. (The Free Dictionary, 1979)

This argument is reinforced by George Herbert Mead who declares that no thinking is possible, and no sense of self, that is, independent of social processes (Gergen, 2010) – as Abercrombie (2004) says, the self is socially constructed – and so is creativity!

Whether or not a product is creative depends on social judgment (Amabile, 1983a, 1983b), which also means that people's understandings of their reality is closely related to their language as "people see and understand the world through the cultural lens of language" (Sapir and Whorf, in Macionis, 2009: 46). A German has different definitions for creativity than an American or a Bolivian does. There are even words in languages that cannot be easily translated. An American interior designer, for example, would not readily understand what a German customer means when she asks for a "gemütlich" living room concept. The word is often translated as "cozy" but it has so many other connotations that there is no equivalent one-word designation in English.

Like the constructionists mentioned, sociologist Collins (1997, 1998) determines that innovation and creativity are products of networks which extend over many pupils and centuries. Others see creativity as craft (Crawford, 2009a, 2009b) where the mastering of tools, good training, learning of domains and fields, rules and contents, and problems and preferences are more important than believing in god-given lightning strikes. And, again, training and mastering of skills, rules, preferences, tastes are all outcomes of social construction of a specific historical time period or Zeitgeist.

A very different explanation for how individuals think about abstract concepts such as creativity is furnished by Wehowsky (1993: 161). Many people want more environmental protection. But a lawyer cannot do more in his daily work than to abide by the law. An economist ignores these concerns as long as they do not impact his budget. A doctor sees environmental problems predominantly as presenting in patients' health, and a chemist recognizes problems only when her readings exceed the maximum allowable values. The individual is separated into the private person who is concerned about issues, and the public person who sees only a slice of them (translation mine). Trying to understand grand systems is impossible in this view, and all subsystems react only to that for which they were created – they cannot react to that which does not exist inside of them. Subsystems are blind to the need of other subsystems, and cannot accommodate the needs of a supersystem (Schrader, 1993: 182–183, translation mine).

The supersystem can be thought of as historically and culturally situated societies, and subsystems as different domains and fields that extract from the supersystem abstract ideas, and then shape their meanings in their respective environments. Integrating *synergetics*, that is, the science of transforming systems, focusing on the total system instead of the small parts that make the whole, could possibly allow insights into self-organizing and self-structuring of the whole, independently of the small parts in creativity. Such a macro approach would look not only at the construction of knowledge in any given society, but also investigate the connection between, for example, economic systems and creativity in different national and cultural contexts, and the influence of such systems on processes of meaning making (e.g., schools and colleges; see also Puccio et al.'s 2012 systems theory). This exploration awaits different emic and etic research in the future.

A novel research approach to the cultural construction of creativity is that of Danish anthropologist Kasper Tang Vangkilde's fieldwork for his dissertation which took place at the German design house Hugo Boss in Switzerland (2012). He found that creativity is not an individual trait but a social process that occurs among individuals. Vangkilde not only kills

DOI: 10.1057/9781137531223.0008

the public sentimental view of the lonely prima donna like Karl Lagerfeld who pours out marvelous designs, through some divine intervention or inborn genius, but also echoes Sawyer's insistence that creativity happens as a result of group effort, where many different players are involved in a creative process (2012: 1). Style meetings, for example, constantly take place at Hugo Boss, involving the creative director just as much as the dressmakers. Unusual about Vangkilde's work is that he helped Hugo Boss learn more about the processes that create its fashion collections, thus enabling optimization. "Every single innovative feature that comes out of a fashion house must match the house's brand" (p. 2), so that "innovation takes place within a specific brand identity, what I call the logic of branding" (p. 3) which Vangkilde found to be a result of designers' "display of extraordinary attention to their surrounding" (p. 3). He calls Hugo Boss "atypical" because the fashion house does not have a top designer whom people equate with the brand such as Lagerfeld for Chanel. Lagerfeld has been highly successful in maintaining the image of an autocratic creative genius (p. 3) suggesting that there is no systemization at Chanel. That, of course, says Vangkilde, is not true – but admitting to it would undermine Lagerfeld's public image!

Cultural contexts are also embedded in different fields which define innovations. Gergen declares that having "functioning communities" requires the constant rebuilding of meaning (2010). The important portion of this term is how creativity has different meanings to the cultural context of a community of advertisers (Lois, 2012) as opposed to the cultural context of a community of graphic designers (Oldach, 1995). In order to understand how creativity is constructed, we need to listen to what different cultures, and fields within them, mean by the term. Products also acquire meaning in different cultural contexts – so unless the entire world is becoming Westernized or Americanized, the same products are not prized universally, and we must pay attention to values and cultures in multinational contexts. This need to emphasize values and cultural contexts is also recognized by a number of other academics.

Integrating culture

In a riveting book which describes his recreation of Darwin's travel around the world, German journalist Jürgen Neffe concludes that

DOI: 10.1057/9781137531223.0008

"[h]umanity owes more than 95% of its existence to this amazing phenomenon called 'culture'" (2008: 464, translation mine). There are several other scholars who are similarly proposing that culture may be as important as, if not more important than, genes in directing our behavior which distinguishes itself in humans in its astonishing ability to adapt (see, especially, Richerson and Boyd, 2005; anthropologist Haviland et al., 2011; Lerner, 2013). For creativity, insights into cultural differences, Segal insists, would be beneficial because "more research and dialogue on cultural definitions of creativity would provide important contributions to a fuller understanding and appreciation of creativity on a global scale" (2000: 12). Implied in this call is also the need to listen more closely to Europeans' bristling critique at American exclusive quantitative methodological approaches in creativity. There has been widespread criticism of US-derived testing models and questioning of whether creativity can even be measured (European Commission, 2009a). Philosophically, the American model implies that creativity cannot exist unless it is measured with an appropriate scale, one that adheres to the demands of validity and reliability. Purser and Montuori (2000) call this "North American bias." A very different approach to conducting creativity research comes from Romanian social-psychologist Glăveanu who emphasizes a broad, micro-macro methodological focus.

Glăveanu (2010) makes the interesting observation that "creativity is prized in almost all cultures, but while Western cultures emphasize the pragmatic, problem-solving outcome of creativity (product), Eastern ones highlight the personal fulfillment of creators (as a form of enlightenment)" (p. 151). Most cross-cultural studies have been criticized for using a "Western (or American) framework, and there are still hardly any high quality *emic* approaches to creativity" (p. 151), so that "simply considering culture as a 'dependent variable' is insufficient" (p. 152). Emic research studies social behavior from the local perspective such as Everett did, accepting, without ethnocentric value judgments, how that society or community lives, thinks, believes, does religion, and so on. It means, in essence, to be or to think like a native. Etic study, on the contrary, looks for general, universal insights, and considers macro structures such as economics. Consistent with the *Sociological Imagination*, a look at how creativity has meaning to members of a community should be accompanied by investigating values that transcend cultures, leading to rich, deep, emic data combined with global, theoretical etic data collection. This necessitates a worldwide network of creativity researchers.

DOI: 10.1057/9781137531223.0008

Feldman similarly sees the need for a cross-cultural account of the concept, that is, "there are indeed certain circumstances in which social/ cultural realities largely determine the possibility or lack of possibility for developing creativity in a given field" (1999: 179). He describes as examples religious groups that forbid girls to learn creative crafts such as music or restrictive systems such as former apartheid South Africa which excluded entire groups from pursuing creative fields.

Esquivel and Peters (1999) point to diversity, bilingualism, cognitive styles, identification, and educational implications as parts of a cultural system while Magyari-Beck (who proposes "creatoloy," "scientometrics," and "creatometrics") looks at culture as a support system for creative products, and creative products in culture as support systems for the survival of social entities; Lubart (1999) dissects the meaning of culture to separate out variables that would function as indicators to measure creativity cross-culturally; and Saad (2009) investigates whether cultures possess traits either promoting or hindering creative thinking.

Lubart acknowledges that "creativity does not occur without a context. The physical and social environment can serve to spark creativity or to squelch it. The environment is also involved in the definition and evalua-tion of creativity" (1990: 39). There are fundamental differences between Eastern and Western conceptions of creativity (i.e., Hinduism, West African Hausa, Chinese), and the importance that is given in Western societies to product – not just the product itself, but the value of the product. "Culture" is used here to denote the idea that Arab communi-ties permit creativity on technical issues, but not religious ones (p. 45). Another observation by Lubart is that creativity may be restricted to status or gender (p. 46) and vary with masculinity or femininity (see Feldman's similar argument earlier). In addition, he notes that language plays a significant role (e.g., Whorf's proposition that language shapes thought, in Lubart, 1990: 47) in what is termed in the present book the 'social construction of creativity'.

The cultural preeminence of American celebration of self-sufficiency, individualism, risk-taking, product, and profit orientation has been challenged by a diverse group of psychology creativity researchers around the world (see Raina's 1999 discussion of cross-cultural differ-ences). Kaufman's and Sternberg's *International Handbook of Creativity* (2006) describes the variety of multicultural assessments of creativity. Fundamentally different definitions of creativity are presented from Scandinavia, China, Taiwan, Hong Kong, Korea, French-speaking

DOI: 10.1057/9781137531223.0008

countries, Israel, German-speaking countries, Poland, Soviet Russia, various African nations, Turkey, Spain, several Latin American nations, and India. As Glăveanu argues, creativity as a process, as a behavior, as an outcome, as desirable is indeed acknowledged globally, but the meanings, the behaviors, the outcomes are culture-specific (2010).

All of the following examples of culturally specific definitions of creativity are taken from Kaufman and Sternberg (2006). Smith and Carlsson say that Scandinavians understand creativity as an attitude toward life, a way to come to grips with the problems of existence, and that there is not as much attention paid to productivity as in America (p. 4); according to Niu, China sees creativity as a component of giftedness and Taiwan profoundly values creative enterprises while Hong Kong celebrates contributions to society's progress (p. 4); Choe (pp. 7–8), on the contrary, shows that Korean interpretations of creativity are heavily influenced by Western, and here especially American, interpretations; French-speaking countries, according to Mouchiroud and Lubart, consider important the four Ps (person, process, product, press, originated by Rhodes, 1961), while German-speaking countries (Preiser) value useful solutions to problems, emphasizing knowledge, experience, abilities, cognitive styles, motive, personality traits, and interests (p. 5). Israelis see as creative the real-world problem solving (Milgram and Livne, 5); Italians (Antonietti and Cornoldi, 6) are focused on Lombroso's interpretations in the past and now are preoccupied with increasing creative performance. Polish researchers are interested in "small c" creativity (Necka, 6) while Soviet Russia (Stepanossova and Grigorenko, 6–7) zeroes in on Gestalt and Marxist psychology.

Creativity is viewed differently in African countries (Mpofu et al., 7) to include innovation, personal agency, social impact, domain-specificity, mysticism, and the imitative, as opposed to Turkey's (Oral, 7) focus on fantasy. In Latin America (Preiss and Strasser, 8), creativity is seen as a multifaceted phenomenon whereas in Spain, research has concentrated since the 1960s on the production of original behavior, models, rules, or objects to solve problems (Genovard et al., 8). In the Far East, India and Hinduism see creativity as human desire for the extension of the self (Misra et al., 9).

One other example for a very different view of creativity is furnished by Kim (2007) who explores the four principles of Confucianism to show how Asian cultures influence creativity. People from Confucian societies seem less creative than Westerners, says Kim, since Confucianism

DOI: 10.1057/9781137531223.0008

may inhibit the development of creative thinking. The four creativity principles emphasized are education, family, hierarchical relationships, and benevolence. Confucianism is a macrocultural element which Kim directly connects to the "so called East-Asian economic miracle" (p. 30). This is contrary to the Western ideas of creativity and includes a creative atmosphere with psychological safety and deferred judgment. To state it differently, the *Five Dragon* societies of Hong Kong, Japan, Singapore, Korea, and Taiwan carry in their cultural Confucian system values such as rote learning which are antithetical to Western creative expression. Equally, Confucianism traditionally emphasizes anti-vocational classicism. It devalues creative product and prizes studies in ethics.

Contrary to especially American cultural values, Confucianism is predominantly concerned with collectivistic norms and authoritarian forms of organization and management. Play, widely considered a cornerstone of creativity, is severely curtailed in East Asian childhood. Important, on the contrary, are filial piety, obedience, and loyalty to the family or company. Kim cites Hwang that "filial piety is so specific to Confucian culture that no comparable concepts can be found in other cultures" (2007: 34). The third principle of Confucianism is based on five codes of ethics which are in turn based pn unequal, but complementary, relationships between people (i.e., ruler/subject, father/son, husband/wife, older/younger brother, and friends) (p. 35). The last principle of Confucianism pertains to benevolence, that is, self-restraint, self-discipline, duty, and the absence of affectionate expression and individuality. Conformity in Western thought is the antithesis of creativity. Conformity is, however, central to Asian societies – think of the Japanese saying that a nail that sticks out needs to be hammered down. These are cultures that devalue almost everything which our Western societies consider important for creativity.

Hempel and Sue-Chan (2010) have found that culture and creativity assessment as determined by communities of experts (in this book: fields) in different spheres (in this book: domains) is one of the first steps in across-culture research that needs to be taken to determine Western and Chinese creativity concepts. They found both similarities and differences, partially directly opposite interpretations. Creativity is hence not one unidimensional "thing," that is, one can see as creative an act or product, but not a social idea (Hempel and Sue-Chan, 2010: 425). Another interesting observation comes from Plafker (2003) who blames the Confucian system for the lack of creativity in academic settings in

DOI: 10.1057/9781137531223.0008

China which groom junior faculty to respect, and defer to, their older faculty and teachers. They are home-grown, in-bred, and sometimes incompetent, he says (translation mine).

For a managerial/organizational perspective, Morris and Leung (2010) report that economic woes have pushed Asian countries from Japan to Singapore, and Taiwan (the so-called Republic of Creativity) to China to question traditional conformity in classrooms and businesses, and have called for a fostering of creativity. Research on differences between Eastern and Western "creative accomplishments," however, could not pinpoint these differences to personality, but rather has singled out norms as one contributing factor. Another factor is centralized control over creativity which is exercised both at the societal and the organizational level (Morris and Leung, 2010).

Anthropologist Everett equally views creativity as culture-specific, where

> The human mind is productive and creative, and language has evolved to express this culturally and psychologically driven creativity. But some researchers have confused the creativity of the mind with the creativity of language. Language itself is not creative. It expresses the creativity of our cultures and brains. Ironically, one of the reasons that kids sound more creative in some ways than adults is because cultures also have a "damping" effect on creativity, reducing it by pressuring members towards conformity as they spend more time in it. (2012: 131)

To Everett, creativity and individuality are two important, but typically Western values (2008).

We need international comparative research to understand these differences outlined previously. When we shift attention from micro (Einstein was creative) to macro (cultural differences), we also shift the definition of creativity. Csikszentmihalyi has proposed that creativity arises from environments, which can be changed to be more creative (1996: 1), but empirical data on this hypothesis are lacking at this time, especially in a multinational context. Giving more weight to the environment could have both theoretical and practical implications for creativity, especially in societies that emphasize creative cultures more than they emphasize creative people. Passoth (2012: 53, translation mine) insists that images of creativity are variable and depend on the changing conditions of modern societies. Creativity is a historically variable phenomenon that changes with the changes in modern societies, with differing relevance (p. 58, translation mine), a process which could take decades.

DOI: 10.1057/9781137531223.0008

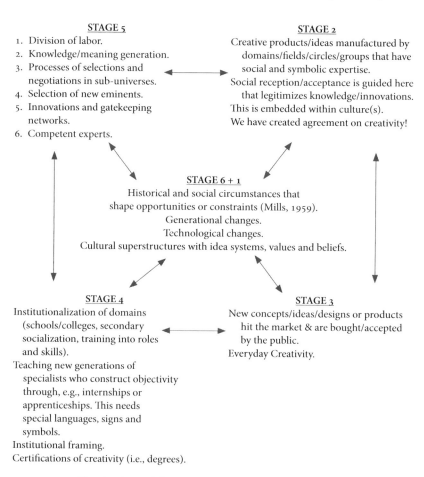

STAGE 5
1. Division of labor.
2. Knowledge/meaning generation.
3. Processes of selections and negotiations in sub-universes.
4. Selection of new eminents.
5. Innovations and gatekeeping networks.
6. Competent experts.

STAGE 2
Creative products/ideas manufactured by domains/fields/circles/groups that have social and symbolic expertise.
Social reception/acceptance is guided here that legitimizes knowledge/innovations.
This is embedded within culture(s).
We have created agreement on creativity!

STAGE 6 + 1
Historical and social circumstances that shape opportunities or constraints (Mills, 1959).
Generational changes.
Technological changes.
Cultural superstructures with idea systems, values and beliefs.

STAGE 4
Institutionalization of domains (schools/colleges, secondary socialization, training into roles and skills).
Teaching new generations of specialists who construct objectivity through, e.g., internships or apprenticeships. This needs special languages, signs and symbols.
Institutional framing.
Certifications of creativity (i.e., degrees).

STAGE 3
New concepts/ideas/designs or products hit the market & are bought/accepted by the public.
Everyday Creativity.

FIGURE 3.1   *The circular social construction of creativity*

So, how is creativity constructed in our Western, individualized societies? The following model represents the circular social construction of creativity.

> We should not forget that it is not always a genius who produces some type of work, but that it is the consumers who create the genius who creates the work. (W. Lange-Eichbaum, 1928, in Brodbeck, 2006 – translation mine)

Stage 6+1 is at the beginning, the end, and the center of the model because it is both influenced by, and in turn influences, all of the stages in the model. Here, we find the social and historical circumstances in any one specific epoch (such as a Renaissance or a society) shaping both our opportunities and constraints as individuals (Mills, 1959). Being a young girl in America means one has opportunities for a formal education, being a young girl in Afghanistan means that one most likely does not. This is the stage in which generational and technological changes construct the cultural superstructure that contains such things as idea systems, values, and beliefs. This stage influences all others around it, but it is, consistent with the Sociological Imagination, mostly hidden from the view and immediate experience of individuals. Vygotsky has pointed out that "every inventor, even a genius, is always the outgrowth of his time and environment" (Sawyer et al., 2003: 78), and the status of being creative is conferred socially, add Sawyer et al., because others, at that same time, determine what is creative. This creative status, however, changes over historical times (81), which is reflected at this stage.

Oelze (2012) has argued that discourses and semantics of creativity are based in various forms of knowledge. They are not inventions of individuals but rather products of interactions. As such, they are bound to historical and societal conditions. Therefore, discourses on creativity are reflections of preferences that are typical for specific social groups (p. 87, translation mine) and, it should be added, cultures.

Stage 6+1 influences, and is also influenced by, new products and ideas (Stage 2), domains, and fields which contain social and symbolic expertise (Stage 3), institutions such as colleges or secondary schools, as well as apprenticeships/internships (Stage 4), and (Stage 5), the one that prepares and implements, through domain and field-specific division of labor, new generations of knowledge and meanings. New idea systems from fields and technological inventions and innovations can occur at any of the stages influencing Stage 6+1.

Several theories support the existence of Stage 6+1 as the one with central influence. Vygotsky (in Gergen, 2010: 92) said that there is nothing in the mind of people that is not first in society. According to Adolf et al., creativity evolves only from society, not in and of itself (2013). They see society serving as the basis for creativity and innovation where environmental, social, and historical factors enhance or suppress not only domains, but also behavior. Tudor (2008) asserts that research from different disciplines has confirmed that creativity exists as a general human behavior as well as a context-dependent behavior attribute. This is here interpreted to mean that the potential for creativity is a capacity situated in human nature (what Marx has called "species being," 1953). However, creativity is also bound to behavioral attributes and definitions that are limited by their context, that is, the specific field or domain humans inhabit, and their gatekeepers.

Stage 6+1 serves as the cultural superstructure which contains specific idea systems, historical, and social circumstances that shape people's opportunities or constraints (think, e.g., of how differently lives are affected when there are wars, or technological revolutions). This stage undergoes not just generational, but also technological changes which fundamentally impact the societies it serves. Idea systems, values, beliefs, Zeitgeist live here, transmitted from one generation to the next.

In Stage 2, the domains/fields/circles and groups in any specific time/epoch develop creative products and ideas which contain social and symbolic expertise (e.g., when Interior Designers declare granite kitchen counters indispensible in an elegant kitchen). At this stage, social reception and acceptance are guided and reinforced, for example, by advertising the advantages of elegant granite kitchen counters. Few customers understand that there have also been disadvantages to granite countertops. It is a high maintenance surface that needs to be regularly treated with a sealant to prevent water infiltration; it is very expensive when compared to other, more durable surfaces; due to its weight, it needs reinforced cabinets; it is porous, which means it easily stains, absorbs water, and even harbors bacteria unless regularly sealed (www.ehow.com/list_6959170_disadvantages-granite-countertops.html). Do the customers who admire these granite countertops on *Home and Garden Television* television shows really know what is in store for them in their kitchen, or do they simply accept the opinion of experts who peddle this product?

Brodbeck's (2006) observation that in modern capitalism, the functional distinction between newness and value is institutionalized and at the same time brutalized fits into this stage. There is a necessity for innovation in each society where new products are subjected to economic determination in competitive open markets (translation mine). This is true of Western industrialized societies just as much as of African tribal markets. Many creatives, says Brodbeck, are keenly aware of the value systems that may prevent innovation so that they bring to the public only those things and products that they believe will be acceptable (translation mine).

According to Gergen, "what we take to be knowledge of the world grows from relationships, and is embedded not within individual minds, but within interpretive or communal traditions" (2010: 88). What constitutes the latest and best in innovation for kitchen counters is agreed

DOI: 10.1057/9781137531223.0008

upon by the field of interior designers and granite stone producers, and a process of moving these new ideas into the popular arena begins (i.e., television shows and magazine articles and phone apps that advertise the newest products). The domains/fields/circles and groups at this stage possess what Sawyer et al. have considered a necessary precondition for constructing creative products/ideas: language, symbols, and tools of the domain (2003). Finally, what is required is social confirmation, that is, validation by experts (Csikszentmihalyi, 1996: 25) for something to be called creative and to move on into the public arena where it is publicized by various media.

Stage 2 is the one that represents the legitimization of knowledge and innovations which have come from Stage 5 and Stage 6+1 since "creative ideas vanish unless there is a receptive audience to record and implement them" (Csikszentmihalyi, 1999: 6). Here, competent outsiders have given approval to new ideas or products, and agreement has been reached over what is considered creative (p. 6). This stage probably comes closest to what Brodbeck (2006) has described as the system models of creativity (represented by Csikszentmihalyi and Amabile) where the creative process appears as a play between environment, person, and domain. What we get, then, are system theoretical aspects, process, product, cultural-social environment with "newness as a criterion" (Torrance in Brodbeck, 2006: 4, translation mine). Newness is, of course, a judgment based in value, which is a reflection of the time and superstructure it is embedded in (Stage 6+1). What individuals consider new is not necessarily new for an entire society, or even globally.

It is what Adolf et al. (2013) have called "knowledgeability," the combination of competencies seen as the foundation for potential innovative thinking, which is present here, in Stage 2, where this knowledgeability has been manufactured by pushing boundaries of rules, having the authority to speak and participate in domains/fields/society, that is, the capacity for mastering personal and professional lives and form social milieus that bring about new ideas (Adolf et al., 2013). Sawyer has called this "situated social nature of creative practices" (2015: xiii). After understanding how various domains and fields reduce creativity (e.g., managers regarding it as productivity and innovation), there is an empty word left in the end which can be used for any purpose (Oelze, 2012: 88, translation mine).

The process of creating agreement on creativity now moves to Stage 3 where the new concept, idea, design, or product hits the popular market.

DOI: 10.1057/9781137531223.0008

The process of meaning making and giving begins, or, as LaChapelle points out, the central question is now whether creative acts are valued (1983: 133). Some of this value may strike us as capricious such as a new type of pizza or yet another iPhone application. The issue in this stage is not objective valuation of the product, but whether or not the public accepts and buys (into) the product or idea. And people, say Littlejohn and Domenici, support what they have created (2000: 53), or what is consistently seen as innovation in the Zeitgeist they live in. One practical example of Littlejohn and Domenici's proposition is the current hype in the United States surrounding the Apple Watch. It has become the latest "have-to-have" thing.

Csikszentmihalyi's idea of *Flow* (1996) suggests that one of the contributing factors of constructing creativity is "clear goals and feedback from other people" so that the outcome or the product is not just accepted by its domain or field in Stage 6+1, but also is considered as useful in Stage 2. When creativity is attributed predominantly to dispositional, not situational, causes (see Kasof, 1999: 147), the contextual influences (also called "social-ecological perspective") facilitate the social reception of the original products by the public (p. 148).

This is the stage where emphasis on economic success as an indicator of creative products or ideas originates. It would be interesting to investigate who decides what is distinctively creative and what is not because those entities are the ones who ultimately decide, together with the gatekeepers, what new knowledge is to be fused into the knowledge base that undergirds Stage 6+1. Innovation is necessary where new products are subjected to economic value determination in the competitive open market (Brodbeck, 2006, translation mine).

Stage 4 is where institutionalization of knowledge and meaning takes place so that the next generation of specialists can be trained and socialized into their roles and skills for the future. Here, objectivity is constructed. We have now accepted new concepts and ideas and designs and see them as objectively creative or desirable. At this stage, languages, signs, and symbols are developed and taught to a new cadre of pupils who will be deemed successful by means of bestowing certificates or titles. Bourdieu has called this stage "cultural capital," that is, the socioeconomic status, good schools, masters, mentors, or coaches so one can learn the symbolic systems and definition of creative products and ideas (1979). The importance of learning is also emphasized by Csikszentmihalyi who say that

DOI: 10.1057/9781137531223.0008

Instructions for how to use fire, or the wheel, or atomic energy are not built into the nervous system of ... children. Each child has to learn them again from the start. The analogy to the genes in the evolution of culture are memes, or units of information that we must learn if culture is to continue. Languages, numbers, theories, songs, recipes, laws and values are all memes that we pass on to our children so that they will be remembered. It is these memes that a creative person changes, and if enough of the right people see the change as an improvement, it will become part of the culture. (1996: 7)

It is at this stage that the history of the domain is taught and skills are transferred from masters to apprentices, or teachers to students. Creative production in this stage requires fluency in languages, symbols, and tools of the domains and fields (Sawyer et al., 2003). John-Steiner observes that creative contributions require mastery of tools and content of the discipline, what she calls "apprenticeships" with highly skilled mentors. Those apprenticeships are not only limited to the arts (e.g., music), but also take place in machine shops tailoring establishments, bakeries, or within families (2015: 36), and new generations subsequently change technologies and come up with new approaches. This concept of apprenticeship is reflected in the model described in Chapter 3, where creativity is embedded within a structure that determines its meaning. Domains, according to John-Steiner (p. 37), retain "funds of knowledge" and pass them on while socializing apprentices into ideologies, processes, and values.

Scheler has posited that "human knowledge is given in society as an a priori to individual expvaerience, providing the latter with its order of meaning" (in Berger and Luckmann, 1967: 8) so that thinking for humans cannot be independent of ideologies and their social contexts (p. 10), which, of course, is learned. Sawyer et al. phrase this differently, that is, "one cannot understand creativity without understanding the field that consists of people who control or influence a domain (e.g., art critics and gallery owners), and which evaluates and selects new ideas" (2003). It is here, in Stage 4, that the new emerging gurus, esteemed scholars, respected leaders emerge, and from where they go on to Stage 5 to participate in the generation of new knowledge and innovation. Hempel and Sue-Chan (2010) propose that since ideas and creativity are domain-dependent, research could evaluate whether innovations, for example, that have a potential of effecting organizational change would be seen as positive or as negative.

Stage 5. "It is easier to enhance creativity by changing conditions in the environment than by trying to make people think more creatively.

And a genuinely creative accomplishment is almost never the result of a sudden insight, a lightbulb flashing on in the dark, but comes after years of hard work" (Csikszentmihalyi, 1996: 1). In this stage, processes of selection take place, and the ideas from a division of labor are negotiated. New stars or superstars are selected in this stage, as are networks for innovation and gatekeeping. Having been trained in schools of thought or networks, these select groups of people now go on not only to construct new knowledge itself, but also select and negotiate with their environments the significance of innovative ideas or extensions of schools of thought.

People and products are "conferred creative status socially ... they are creative because others, at a certain time, think they are creative. This creative status changes over historical times" (Sawyer et al., 2003: 81). Social confirmation is thus necessary for something to be called creative, and therefore needs validation by competent experts, what Csikszentmihalyi calls "external confirmation" (1996: 25). Creative ideas vanish unless there is a receptive audience to record and implement them (p. 6). Thus, "creativity results from the interaction of a system composed of three elements: a culture that contains symbolic rules, a person who brings novelty into the symbolic domain, and a field of experts who recognize and validate the innovation. All three are necessary for a creative idea, product, or discovery to take place" (p. 6). In addition, Vygotsky has commented that most eminent are those creators who best utilize the social and cultural tools and best fit with the social and cultural expectations of their time (Sawyer et al., 2003: 80).

Critics of social constructionism

There are, of course, critical voices surrounding social construction arguments. Ian Hacking (1999) is one of those, as is Thomas Luckmann (2013, personal e-mail exchanges) and Langdon Winner (1993). Hacking, for example, in his "sticking points" discussion, refers to issues of contingency, nominalism, and stability. Things could be otherwise than they are, our realities could be very different if we chose to make them such, and meaning changes all the time! The stability of knowledge is, indeed, the result of external factors which include institutionalization, social networks, eminents, Zeitgeist, history, and idea systems.

DOI: 10.1057/9781137531223.0008

Luckmann, in his 2008 *Constitution, Construction* states that he wants to emphasize unmistakenly that when he and Berger published *The Social Construction of Reality*, they *could not* have known, and nowadays do *not want* to know, about later epistemologically and theoretically untenable developments in constructionism/constructivism (p. 33). He is a critic of Gergen's social constructionist approach (2013, personal e-mail exchange). For a detailed account of constructionism critiques, see also Stam's (2001) edited volume and article on the subject in *Theory and Psychology*. In his Introduction, Stam briefly maps out the various arguments against Gergen's position that range from accusations of internal contradictions to objectivism being inherently authoritarian, from constructionist scientists being constructionist about descriptions instead of the subject matter of the construction, from realism to antirealism (pp. 291–296).

The following chapter shifts gears from the theoretical (and its critiques) to the empirical. What began as a small exploratory inquiry, an attempt at what Max Weber called "Verstehen," has become a large research project with no end in sight. "Verstehen" as a methodological process seeks to understand how people attach meaning to their social worlds, that is, how their realities are being constructed by them. So, how do different groups of people define what creativity is for them?

DOI: 10.1057/9781137531223.0008

4

Research Results

Abstract: *What began as a curious inquiry into the meaning of a concept has mushroomed into a longitudinal project with a qualitative-quantitative methodological ("triangulation") approach. Several methodologies were employed over six years to gauge the expectations of the students of an applied art and design school as well as those of employers and industry professionals. The differences are striking: while students (N=1,724) expect to be able to use their creativity by working independently, employers and industry professionals (N=533) have much less use for creative thinking in general, and are, instead, focused on behavioral issues such as punctuality, reliability, honesty, and so on. The students have unrealistic expectations of their future work environments just as employers and industry professionals have unrealistic expectations of their future workforce. What role should education play in this, and how important is creativity in people's work?*

Reuter, Monika E. *Creativity – A Sociological Approach.*
Basingstoke: Palgrave Macmillan, 2015.
DOI: 10.1057/9781137531223.0009.

An exploratory study

This chapter describes the longitudinal triangulation research project (inspired by Babbie, 2010) that began in the Fall of 2009. The project is ongoing, and the results presented here are reflective of only a partial analysis of data. There are two more research approaches planned for the future, that is, a content analysis of courses on creativity taught onground and via MOOCs (Massive Open Online Courses), and a participant observation in a creative occupation – at either an advertising agency or a design firm.

In November 2009, an open-ended questionnaire was administered to a convenience sample of students at The Art Institute of Fort Lauderdale (N=124) asking them for their definitions of creativity. In January 2010, during one of the college's all school meetings, a focus group with faculty members was conducted (N=24), asking the same question, that is, what does creativity mean to you? From February to June 2010, students in several *Research Methods* classes served as three focus groups (N=60) answering the question, "What is Creativity?" *Research Methods* students in subsequent classes then operationalized the concept based on the feedback from the open questionnaire and the focus groups, and helped to construct a survey. This survey was administered to both randomly selected classes (both program and General Education courses), and convenience samples (i.e., students in lower-level introductory and senior-level portfolio classes) by the author and other faculty. Because the college is privately owned, there was no access to the student data base, which made traditional random selection of a sample impossible. Alternatively, a random sample of classes from among the more than 500 sections taught at the time was chosen by *Research Methods* classes, and those students administered the surveys in those sections. At the times when surveys were administered, the student population at the college varied from 2,500 to 2,800. A total of 1,724 surveys were collected over two years. The results of this survey, based originally on a five-point Likert scale, are shown here:

Results of Student Surveys, N=1,724

1. I am
   Male   41%   Female   55%

2. I am in my (_) term
   First   33%   Third   22%
   Second 26%   Fourth   15%

DOI: 10.1057/9781137531223.0009

Responses are aggregated into three major categories (not likely, neutral, likely), from a previous five-item Likert scale (i.e., least likely, less likely, neutral, more likely, and most likely). The "no answer" variable was removed, hence percentages do not necessarily add up to 100.

How I feel more likely to be creative is:

	1 (%) Least/Not likely	2 (%) Neutral	3 (%) More/Most likely
3. By myself	6%	21%	73%
4. In a group	16%	30%	51%
5. When I do personal art	9%	16%	73%
6. When I do commercial art for work	17%	32%	50%
7. When I have to solve a problem	11%	25%	64%
8. When I do something new	6%	19%	74%
9. When I follow process and procedure	27%	32%	40%
10. When I have the freedom to create	3%	9%	88%
11. Anybody can be creative	20%	25%	55%
12. When I have passion	2%	5%	92%
13. When I have to improvise	10%	23%	66%
14. When I have a project that I need to spend time and energy on	7%	21%	70%
15. Can hands-on activities in the class-room or at work improve creativity?	4%	14%	80%
16. Bright, colorful classroom	16%	28%	56%
17. Playing games with students in a class	20%	31%	49%
18. A project done by the entire class	25%	26%	48%
19. Doing experiments (doodle projects, building something in class from paper/clay/etc.)	9%	20%	71%
20. By teaching concepts for innovation	6%	24%	70%

In my opinion, the statements below are least or most likely

	1 (%) Least/Not likely	2 (%) Neutral	3 (%) More/Most likely
21. Practicing the process/technique	6%	20%	73%
22. Every person has a creative side	12%	18%	70%
23. Creativity means that you have to work on your abilities	17%	26%	58%
24. Creativity is most likely found in groups	33%	35%	32%
25. Creativity is not the same as problem solving	29%	28%	42%

DOI: 10.1057/9781137531223.0009

The following responses from this survey stand out:

▸ question # 3: 73% of the students stated that they are more or most likely to be creative by themselves;
▸ question # 5: 73% of the students stated that they are more or most likely to be creative when they do personal art;
▸ question # 10: 88% of the students stated that they are more or most likely to be creative when they have the freedom to create;
▸ question # 12: 92% of the students stated that they are more or most likely to be creative when they have passion;
▸ question # 20: 70% of the students stated that they are more or most likely to be creative when being taught concepts for innovation; and
▸ question # 22: 70% of the students stated that it is more or most likely that every person has a creative side.

Students' opinions, however, are only one side of the issue concerning creativity in the workplace.

Electronic interviews with employers and industry professionals

The next phase of the project concentrated on employers and industry professionals. Consistent with the assumption discussed earlier in this book, that creativity is important on the job, feedback from employers and industry professionals was sought to compare to students' opinions on the significance of creativity in their occupations. In addition, Grant (2011) have said that "creativity is the currency of societal progress and the hallmark of success in organizations. To innovate, adapt, excel, and survive, organizations depend on creativity from employees" (p. 1).

Originally, five interviews were conducted in person, but it became obvious very quickly that this way of data collection was both time-consuming and expensive (i.e., taking interviewees to lunch). An open-ended interview was then constructed by a *Research Methods* class into an electronic format, and subsequently e-mailed to approximately 300 employers who routinely hire the college students. The response rate was below 10%, and this data collection procedure was abandoned. Next, approximately 80 Professional Advisory Committee (PAC) members were contacted by e-mail, but again, the response rate was too low (i.e., only 3 PAC members responded). Subsequently, a snowball sampling

DOI: 10.1057/9781137531223.0009

procedure was adopted, where employers and industry professionals were contacted through the college and then recommended others for electronic interviews. For five extra credit points, students in *Research Methods* classes have been collecting one interview from somebody they knew, who is either an employer or an industry professional.

Employers and industry professionals come from a variety of industries in the fashion, video, web, marketing, advertising, graphic design, public relations, television and radio, and the culinary field. They include creative directors, image consulting, and styling experts as well as vice presidents of national and international advertising agencies, and owners of both large and small firms. The students, however, did not limit themselves to the design world and returned electronic interviews by people not connected to design fields at all (e.g., the owner of a small flower shop, sous-chefs, small business owners, academics, general managers, teachers, lawyers, office managers, etc.). Also, interviewees responded from different parts of the world (Australia, India, Europe, Saudi-Arabia, South America).

The number of electronic interviews collected by March 2015 is 533. General results of the interviews are summarized into the following list of skills employers/industry professionals said they are looking for (in order of importance):

The ten skills employers/industry professionals are looking for in employees

1 Program Skills – craft, knowledge of tools, following the processes of the field
2 Work Process Skills – "reality," that is, how employers want jobs done, knowledge about how businesses operate in general
3 Business Skills – administration, budgets, management, problem solving
4 Professional Behavioral Skills – punctuality, reliability, honesty
5 General Skills – English, research, math, public speaking, computer skills, foundation skills
6 Teamwork Skills – prima donnas not welcome, importance of groups/teams, ability to work with others, cooperation instead of competition
7 Client-centered Skills – "the client is always right because s/he is paying the bills"
8 Immersion Skills – passion, dedication, commitment to the profession
9 Boundary-Spanning Skills – interdisciplinary knowledge
10 Ability to accept professional critiques

DOI: 10.1057/9781137531223.0009

tally to the six questions which highlight the importance of creativity (or, rather, the lack thereof!) in the workplace, which are presented in the following pages. Since answers were grouped into several response categories, the numbers of responses for each question do not add up to the number of interviews analyzed so far, that is, a respondent may have said that s/he considers important punctuality, reliability, and communication skills, so this one response was counted in the three subcategories of punctuality, reliability, and communication skills.

What other things do you consider important when you hire for a job?

1   Reliability: 265 = 49.7%
2   Teamwork: 232 = 43.5%
3   Communication skills: 211 = 39.6%
4   Punctuality: 164 = 30.8%
5   Ethical behavior (i.e., truthful, honest, loyalty, accountability, integrity, dedication, pride in work/trust): 93 = 17.4%

People in my business work predominantly:

▶ In teams: 169 = 42.25%
▶ Both in teams and on their own: 121 = 30.25%
▶ On their own: 77 = 22%
▶Depends on the department/project: 6 = 1.5%

What do you consider important for the school to emphasize in students' education?: (interviews # 1–350)

1   Social/interpersonal communication skills: 112 = 32%
2   English/professional communication training & analytical skills: 73 = 20.86%
3   Math and logic/finance/analytical: 64 = 18.29%
4   The real world (e.g., the college's honor group, internships, people skills, face-to-face, and verbal communication/interpersonal skills): 38 = 10.86%
5   Administrative skills, know how to run a day-to-day office/business and management skills/business etiquette/taxes: 35 = 10%
6   Well-rounded, that is, reading/critical thinking/science/history/ literature/general education/social sciences/geography: 25 = 7.14%

DOI: 10.1057/9781137531223.0009

7 (Advanced) computer/technical skills (Adobe)/design/software: 21 = 6%
8 Professionalism/get the job done/ability to deal with change/ attitude: 14 = 4%
9 Teamwork/team effectiveness: 11 = 3.14%
10 Responsibility/work ethics: 8 = 2.29%
11 Creativity: 7 = 2%

Are principles/process/skills/craft more important than creativity? (interviews # 1–400)

1 Yes, skills/process are more important than creativity: 166 = 41.5%
2 It's a combination of both/they are the same/we need both: 143 = 35.75%
3 Creativity is more important than skills/process: 46 = 11.5%

Would you rather hire a super-talented prima donna, or a less creative, but humble and reliable person? (interviews # 1–400)

▸ Humble: 249 = 62.25%
▸ Prima Donna: 59 = 14.75%
▸ Both: 33 = 8.25%
▸ Depends on the position that needs to be filled: 22 = 5.5%

How can the college better prepare students? (interviews # 1–350)

1 English, writing, and grammar skills: 193 = 55.14%
2 Teamwork: 82 = 23.43%
3 Communication skills: 56 = 16%
4 Real-world experience/externships/internships: 40 = 11.43%
5 Math/financial aspects of the business: 28 = 8%
6 Technical skills/MACs/web design/computer/knife skills/ functionality and not pretty/Microsoft Office/powerpoints/ Excel/social media/mechanical engineering/social media/web development: 25 = 7.14%
7 Business/entrepreneurship skills/marketing/selling/bookkeeping/ public relations: 17 = 4.86%
8 Creativity: 15 = 4.29%
9 Professionalism: 14 = 4%
10 Work ethics: 8 = 2.29%

DOI: 10.1057/9781137531223.0009

Analysis of students versus employers/industry professionals

A comparison of the responses by employers and industry professionals reveals that students and employers/industry professionals are at the opposite ends of the scale in their views concerning several statements described earlier, while they agree on the issue of needing passion in order to be creative. Employers and industry professionals, however, have a very different view of the necessity for creativity on the job.

K. Fischer (2013), in a Special Report on "The Employment Mismatch", found some of the same results as the data reported here, among them that "internships make the difference" (p. 1). This is consistently emphasized by employers and industry professionals who overwhelmingly recommend that students get "real-world experience" before entering the job market. According to Fischer, employers want effective communication (p. 1) and have an expectation that new employees are coming to the job ready to handle duties immediately. Furthermore, in both Fischer's and the current research study, employers complain that colleges in general do not prepare students sufficiently in writing, oral communication, decision making, analytical/research skills, and the capacity to work within a team.

The results of the current study presented here mirror some of Fischer's findings. The most striking differences between students and employers are their respective completely opposite expectations of students' work "in the real world." Students overwhelmingly believe that they can be most creative if they are left alone and have freedom on the job (88%), which is, of course, unrealistic: 70% of the students say that everybody has a creative side, but only 58% think that they have to work on their abilities. Only 32% of students see creativity as being found in groups.

On the opposite end of this spectrum are the employers and industry professionals, most of whom state that their employees work predominantly in groups, or both in groups and by themselves. "Creativity" as a desirable skill, interestingly, does not even appear among the five most important things when hiring for a job, and is a mere # 11 in the list of what they consider important for the school to emphasize in students' education. Among the skills considered important for colleges to prepare students, creativity ranks eighth.

Employers and industry professionals expect from colleges that they "bake" their students ready to hit the ground, not just well prepared in their major, but also well socialized. Some of these expectations are simply unrealistic, that is,

▶ "teach them intuition";
▶ "teach them reality" and politeness;
▶ "teach them maturity" and good etiquette;
▶ "teach them self-assuredness and the will to work hard";
▶ teach them a good work ethic and to always be punctual and prepared
▶ teach them humility;
▶ teach them to respect authority;
▶ teach them to respect diversity;
▶ teach them to think critically – but not too much!
▶ teach them to be well-rounded;
▶ teach them leadership qualities, that is, "as a corporation, we do not want to have to pay for that, and would rather that people already came like that from college";
▶ teach them more energy;
▶ teach them to be willing to do whatever whenever it is expected;
▶ teach them to have a "grounded ego";
▶ teach them to accept critiques; and
▶ teach them to never leave the office before their boss does;

What employers want are good little working ants. What students want is freedom, to work alone, passion, doing something new.

People are not creativity friendly, asserts Olien (2013), because of the pressures to conform and fear of uncertainty. In addition, organizational behavior researcher Staw has found that decisions in organizations are based on anticipating the preferences of those who will be evaluating them (in Olien, 2013: 3), which may render much creative thinking useless. Mangan (2012) believes that there is a disconnect between millions of college graduates and companies that cannot fill jobs with qualified/skilled employees. One of the reasons is that industries and employers increasingly expect colleges to provide on-the-job training through donated equipment or internships. It is not a lack of skills on the part of students, he insists, as much as it is employers not willing to pay for training that is partially to blame for the disconnect. One of the reasons for this may be that employers believe that technology is all around and readily available, and that it is the students' responsibility to seek out and get the training they need. Another reason for this disconnect is lack of communication between schools and employers. Moreover, students and graduates are considered by employers, managers, and industry professionals to be "clueless" about the realities of job requirements and, especially, salaries.

Oelze (2012) furnishes an interesting critique: creativity has the function of stabilizing the social system because if its meaning were clearly determined, people would be able to see through the empty rhetoric and realize that creativity is hardly ever expected in the real world (p. 89, translation mine). The economy does not look for creative power, but to merely sustain a system of effective exploitation of resources, profits, and monopolies (p. 89, translations mine). Creativity in this view turns into a tool of evaluation and domination.

The results from the current research mirror a 2007 survey conducted among 155 superintendents in schools and 89 employers . Many people have suggested that creativity is key for a 21st-century workforce, but educators and executives differ on what specific skills are most important. The 11 abilities considered important by businesses/employers and superintendents are listed in the order of their importance (one most important, ten least important):

	Businesses/ Employers	School Superintendents
Problem identification and articulation	1	9
ID new patterns of behavior or new combination of actions	2	3
Integration of knowledge across different Disciplines	3	2
Originate new ideas	4	6
Comfort with the notion of "no right answer"	5	11
Fundamental curiosity	6	10
Originality and inventiveness in work	7	4
Problem solving	8	1
Ability to take risk	9	8
Tolerance of ambiguity	9	7
Communicate new ideas to others	11	5

(http://www.creativityland.ca/wp-content/uploads/2010/05/what-creativity-implies.jpg)

Again, the disconnect is striking.

Much research is left to be done in order to untangle expectations from different groups concerning creativity, which so many people consider important in a future workforce. Finding "the new" has become a central rhetorical motif in Western societies' science, politics, and economy critiques (Reichertz, 2012, translation mine), and how this translates into expectations in the world of work would be a topic worth researching. How is "the constant construction of novelty socially organized?" (Valsiner et al., 2015: xix).

Another interesting question awaiting further inquiry is where the notion of "shared meaning" comes from, and how successful creativity arises through individuals' maneuvering inside of worlds that are shaped by domains. Glăveanu and Gillespie (2015: 13) say that the "characteristic feature ... (of creativity)" is not the often cited achievement of novelty or usefulness, but "that of *negotiating differences and acting upon*" (p. 13) our world so that it is the process of making the meaning of creativity (Wagoner, 2014: 27) that needs to be studied. In addition, "the reason why creativity is considered a value in contemporary societies (is that) it produces novelty by joining together areas of experience, including cultural artifacts that were previously kept apart" (Valsiner et al., 2015: xix), and produces other odd reshaping of meaning such as "a computer hacker (who) becomes 'creative' after she has become an employee of a software company. Before that, she is a common criminal" (p. xix).

What does all of this mean? What are the implications of the theoretical model, and the empirical data so far collected? What should be done to reconceptualize what different communities of scholars, business owners, the public, creative professionals, and students expect from creativity in their jobs or even in their lives? Valsiner et al. have called for "building new theoretical, methodological, and practical tools for the study of creativity as a socio-cultural phenomenon" (2015: xx) because "creativity does matter ... and ... it is not a separate, but an integral part of our everyday existence" (p. xxii). Some of the questions that should be asked as a consequence of the present research, for example, are whether schools should redesign their curricula to meet employers' and industry professionals' expectations, or whether academics need to educate the business world about the necessity for creativity, and room to grow it, especially for the workforce of the future?

DOI: 10.1057/9781137531223.0009

Conclusion – Homo Creativus: Creamus – Ergo Sumus (We Create – Therefore We Are) or: Sumus – Ergo Creamus? (We Are – Therefore We Create)

Abstract: *The conclusion picks up on the question of the previous chapter – how important creativity is in people's work –and reiterates that the field of Sociology could and should make contributions to the discussion on creativity. The goal of the book to include Sociology in the creativity discussion is briefly discussed again, and the new, predominantly European social-psychological interpretations are outlined. The shortcomings of the research project are presented, alongside questions for further inquiry culled from psychological and social psychological as well as sociological considerations. Are people human because they are creative, or are they creative because they are human? This is a question that has yet to be tackled theoretically. This chapter concludes with the insistence that creativity is socially constructed.*

Reuter, Monika E. *Creativity – A Sociological Approach.* Basingstoke: Palgrave Macmillan, 2015. DOI: 10.1057/9781137531223.0010.

DOI: 10.1057/9781137531223.0010

Humans are, by definition, at their core creative creatures (Ward, 2010)

"As we strive to create a more civil public discourse, a more adaptable and creative workforce, the humanities and social sciences are the heart of the matter," reads *The Heart of the Matter* report (2013) prepared by the Congressional National Commission on the Humanities and Social Sciences headed by Duke University president Richard Brodhead (American Academy of Arts and Sciences, 2013). Although Dr. Brodhead and the commission are concerned about "serious consequences to U.S. security and prosperity" unless "humanities and social sciences are strengthened," their use of the word "creative" is intriguing not just in terms of civil public discourse, but also to describe the contemporary workforce.

This focus on creativity as an important requirement for tomorrow's workforce is echoed by an IBM Global CEO study which found that more than 1,500 chief executive officers from 60 countries and 33 industries around the world selected creativity as the "most crucial factor for future success" (2010). Creativity in this context means the successful navigation of complex environments, which includes relying on ambiguity, innovative models, and global thinking, "creativity as raw material" (Krämer, 2012: 110, translation mine). Yet, Oelze charges that organizations lie when managers talk about, or expect from their employees, creativity because modern corporations, highly rationalized and effective, are the enemy of creative potentials (p. 96, translation mine).

The contribution this book hopes to make to the field of creativity study is based in Sociology whose interpretation of creativity as socially constructed was influenced by various theoretical propositions: Vico's declaration "verum ipsum factum," that is, the true is made, which means that something is true *because* it is made (Bergin and Fisch, 1968); a Marxist interpretation, which means that creativity does not make humans, humans make creativity; Vygotsky's assertion that creativity is fundamental to the development of all individuals, and reveals humans' true nature (1971); Csikszentmihalyi's idea that creativity is a central source of meaning in our lives (1996: 1) and when we are involved in it, we are living more fully than during the rest of our lives (p. 2); Maslow's (1999) suggestion that boldness, courage, freedom, spontaneity, self-acceptance, and self-actualization should be taking place for every human being in a supportive, evaluation-free environment; May's idea

DOI: 10.1057/9781137531223.0010

that humans express their being by creating (1975); Joas' proposition that it is creativity that plays an ever-increasing role in the understanding of contemporary societies (in Sales et al., 2007: 1); Fisher and Lerner's (2013) insistence on social justice that promotes positive human development; Feinstein's 2006 theory of the nature of creative development; and, especially, the officially dead, but ongoing debate over nature versus nurture as described by Overton (in Lerner, 2013) and Richerson and Boyd (2005).

Sociology adds to the field with the proposition that creativity in itself does not actually exist, but rather that it is a social construction – formed and defined in the various domains and fields that make up societies. Although creativity is sought after and desirable, especially in Western capitalist societies, it is also put together and put forward and shaped by the culture that praises it, according to that culture's beliefs and ideals. Fundamental in this process are various stages that are involved in the structuring of creativity.

The model proposed in Chapter 3 suggests that creativity is constructed in the public, schools, universities, professional organizations, specialized languages, signs and framing, generation of meaning, selection of eminents and gatekeepers and experts, and finally in the production of social acceptance and reception.

The most important aspect of this model is culture. "Culture" here means not just different value systems across different national boundaries, but also the content of specific domains and fields which generate their individual cultures and meaning systems. The term also embodies a much broader, overarching meaning, that is, "Cultural psychologists have shown that human behaviour is culturally organized, its development dependent on the culture and structure of the situation" (Jovchelovitch, 2015: 76). This represents the notion of the "profound cultural basis of human creativity" (Baerveldt and Cresswell, 2015: 95) It is predominantly social psychologist Glăveanu who has led the way to viewing creativity from a sociocultural perspective, away from its historically traditional focus on individuals or products.

The discipline of Sociology offers to take a critical look at the superstructure undergirding the meaning-making of creativity. That aspect of creativity has so far not been pursued, even though a superstructure, with its many interpretations and critiques, is always implied in discussions on what creativity is. Geertz (in Baerveldt and Cresswell, 2015: 101) has said that "man is an animal suspended in webs of significance he himself has spun." Sociology should investigate not just what animal is suspended, but what kinds of webs of significance man has spun, how man did it, why, when, and in which historical time. And, by the way, where are all of the sides of the web anchored, and what materials were used?

Before more research is undertaken, and more questions are asked, however, it is prudent to list the shortcomings of not only the model presented in Chapter 3, but also the research project mapped out in Chapter 4. The model is too complex for empirical testing (see also Reuter, 2015). However, as Torlina has pointed out (2013, personal e-mail exchange), the way in which Sociology studies the world is often too simplistic to handle complex grand topics such as creativity. For many sociologists and other social scientists, one of the biggest problems with this model will be its nonlinearity and the fact that it does not present a deductive mode which typically presents causal relationships (Torlina, 2013, personal e-mail exchange). None of the variables contained in the model can be easily defined as dependent or independent. They are all connected to one another. It is also acknowledged that the data presented in Chapter 4 are situation-specific culturally and organizationally (Torlina, 2013, personal e-mail exchange). Consistent with the argument of social construction, however, creativity is limited to, and shaped by, the parameters of our culture and institutional contexts. The concept cannot be reduced to (especially culturally) a specific definition, which is one reason why there are so many definitions of creativity in the literature. If our world indeed requires creative thinking, then we must acknowledge, and not just theoretically, the complexity and messiness (Torlina, 2013, personal e-mail exchange) of the concept and its outcomes.

We need to tease out and possibly settle opposite propositions such as Klausen's (2010) suggestion that the product, not the person or process, be viewed as the primary bearer of creativity. His critique is that "some influential theorists make creativity too strongly dependent on social acceptance" (2010: Abstract). Weissman furnishes the opposite sugges-tion (p. 222), "'process, not product' is a creativity cliché (that) is also a great truth." If the suggestion that creativity is socially constructed can be accepted, then Rusch (2010) is right that creativity and innovation potential should be available to all people – from art to design to craft to scientific discoveries, industries and economies (translation mine), but what does that mean, who can make this possible, and how?

Krämer has found that the capacity for creativity is not an egalitarian talent of all actors, but is used as a criterion for professional differentiation

DOI: 10.1057/9781137531223.0010

in an organization (i.e., the advertising/creative agency where he did his research), and is thus qualified as a creative arena of competence; it also differentiates among people, which results in stratification (2012, translation mine). The fabrication of creativity is, thus, and without doubt, connected to power and status issues. It should be investigated by Sociology to identify practices that are part of daily creativity production (2012, translation mine). This echoes Brooks' observation that "creativity is seen as the new key to productivity, having replaced the Organization Man's virtue, efficiency" (2000: 130). Oelze similarly argues that creativity is now part of one's human capital, a thing of individualism that is responsible for occupational success, and societal roots of failure are thereby excluded. One may fail at this attempt of showing special talent for creativity because one may not be able to fulfill an expectation to deliver something that has no clear definition (2012: 89, translation mine).

Philosophy and anthropology consider among the most precious human capacities the potential for creativity, and at present, that potential for creativity in our educational or occupational arenas in Western industrialized societies is not sufficiently nurturing. It is easier, and less costly to these societies, to produce the good little working ants many employers and industries want than it is to facilitate the shaping of human beings/students/workers whom Maslow, May, Marx, Csikszentmihalyi have in mind. In this context, the question also needs to be addressed: whether industries and employers really do want creative thinking in their employees, or, as the present research suggests, whether job-specific desirable behavior is preferred over the birthing of creative ideas. There are many misconceptions to be cleared up on all sides of the employer/worker divide.

Another way to reshape, especially in the general public, thinking about creativity is to elevate cultural factors to the same rank that psychological theories of innateness have held for the past 65 years. Csikszentmihalyi has made this point:

> Instructions for how to use fire, or the wheel, or atomic energy are not built into the nervous system of the children after such discoveries. Each child has to learn them again from the start. The analogy to genes in the evolution of culture are memes, or units of information that we must learn if culture is to continue. Languages, numbers, theories, songs, recipes, laws and values are all memes that we pass on to our children so that they will be remembered. It is these memes that a creative person changes, and if enough of the right people see the change as an improvement, it will become part of the culture. (1996: 7)

During the keynote address for the eighth biennial meeting of the Society for the Study of Human Development conference in Fort Lauderdale (November, 2013), developmental psychologist Lerner (2013) proposed three interesting ideas: (1) that the key lens through which to see the future in developmental science is social justice; (2) that "the sun has set on split, reductionist accounts stressing nature or nurture"; and (3) that culture is one of the important dimensions of evolution. Individuals have to be viewed within their social contexts, where genes are the followers of culture, that is, emergent social interactions mobilize due to epigenetic developments. For an outstanding argument that bridges biology and culture, see Richerson and Boyd (2005). According to Overton (in Lerner, 2013), the Cartesian scientific paradigm has failed, and we need to change to sensitive methodologies that are longitudinal and multidisciplinary in order to understand community, context, and culture. This would include a new way of conceptualizing creativity.

Two more points from Lerner's presentation warrant mentioning, that is (1) Fisher's ten priorities in her vision for a research agenda for developmental science where number one is "to create and evaluate empirically based interventions that promote a just society that nurtures life-long health development in all of its citizens" (2013), and from Lerner's conclusions, that (2) "the scientific and societal value on which the developmental science of the post-2025 era will be judged will be whether its theoretical and methodological tools are productive at promoting positive human development across the life span for the diverse people of the world" (2013). Positive human development which societies can promote and actively help to construct includes the potential for human creativity. And human creativity, according to Csikszentmihalyi, has to be acquired through training (1996: 50) where rules and content of the domain have to be learned, just as the criteria and selection and the preferences of the field (pp. 47–48).

As a sociological approach, this book has been interested in investigating how creativity was addressed by various domains in the past, and to propose a new way of looking at it. The predominant concern here was what creativity means to different groups of people, specifically, students and employers/industry professionals, and how its meaning is shaped in social processes of fields and domains and products. If creativity is, indeed, the core competency for this millennium, and creative response is more important in individuals' success and satisfaction than any data or technology (Meyer, 2000), then Pink (2010) is correct that

DOI: 10.1057/9781137531223.0010

humans are not horses but that we seek interesting things that give our life meaning! Whether this meaning is experienced in our personal life or in our work, how it is provided from our environments, whether it is an outcome of cultural norms or organizational variables is a question that needs to be posed in empirical research – as Gläveanu has proposed (2014b), with both etic and emic studies. Part of that research should include a theoretical treatise on the question whether creativity is part of human nature, and whether we are creative because we are human, or whether we are human because we create.

Sociology asks: does creativity differ in Western industrialized societies from the rest of the world? How so? What is the influence of the prevailing economic or cultural system? Gender? Age? Politics? How is creativity constructed in various domains and fields? Who are the people who become the creativity leaders? How were they chosen, and how do they choose? Are there gendered creative occupations? If yes, how so and why? What does creativity mean to/for people? Sociology should ask: which practices, mechanisms, and principles are involved in the making of a product that is designed as creative? This necessitates analyses in organizational fields (such as Vangkilde, 2012; Krämer, 2012). How does work in specifically designated creative work environments (e.g., design or advertising agencies) differ (or not?) from creative work in regular work environments? Such research has so far been missing in sociological research (Krämer, 2012, translation mine).

There is a need for quantitative and qualitative research in interdisciplinary approaches to the study of creativity worldwide. The prevailing lore especially in the general public of Western industrialized societies is wrong according to a sociological interpretation: *IT* does not exist at all – *IT* comes into being depending on judgment, evaluation, and importance within the social and cultural circumstances that give rise to *IT*. We make *IT* up. We invent *IT*. We make *IT* real.

DOI: 10.1057/9781137531223.0010

Appendix: Creativity How-to-Books

Adams, J. 2001. *Conceptual Blockbusting* (4th ed.)
Cambridge, MA: Perseus Publishing.

AdvertisingAge. 2012. The Creativity 50. Meet the Minds
Spreading Happiness, Brewing the Next Great Craft
Beer, Beautifying Data, Diversifying the Demographics
of Tech, Saving Lives, Reimagining Magazines,
Sidestepping the Gatekeepers. Cover page, July 9.

Barez-Brown, C. 2008. *How to Have Kick-Ass Ideas*. New
York, NY: Skyhorse Publishing.

Birkenmeyer, B. & Brodbeck, H. 2010a. Innovation ist
fuehrbar! In *Wunderwaffe Innovation: Was Unternehmen
unschlagbar macht – ein Ratgeber fuer Praktiker.* Zürich,
Switzerland: Orell Fuessli Verlag.

Birkenmeyer, B. & Brodbeck, H. 2010b. Stellschraube
Innovationsinstrumente. Auf die Anwendung kommt
es an! *Wunderwaffe Innovation: Was Unternehmen
unschlagbar macht – ein Ratgeber fuer Praktiker.* Zürich,
Switzerland: Orell Fuessli Verlag.

Black, R. A. 2011. If You Can Hold a Pencil, a Pen,
a Crayon or Piece of Chalk, You Can Think and
Generate Ideas Visually, presentation at the American
Creativity International Conference, Fort Lauderdale,
FL, March 31/April 1.

Böttcher, F. 2010. Die Entwicklung radikaler Innovationen
in Innovationsnetzwerken. In P. Harland & M.
Schwarz-Geschka (Eds.), (551–570), op.cit.

DOI: 10.1057/9781137531223.0011

Brodbeck, K-H. 2006. Neue Trends in der Kreativitaetsforschung. *Psychologie in Oesterreich*, 4 & 5: 246–253.

Cameron, J. 2002. *Walking in This World: The Practical Art of Creativity*. New York, NY: Jeremy P. Tarcher/Putnam.

Carter, D. (Ed.). 2005. *Creativity 34: Bright Ideas in Advertising and Design from around the World*. China: Collins Design.

Clausen, T. 2010. Paradigmenwechsel: Von Forschung und Entwicklung zu Connect + Develop – ein Praxisbeispiel von Wella/P&G. In P. Harland & M. Schwarz-Geschka (Eds.), (211–221), op.cit.

Cooper, A. 2010. Chef Jose Andres' Culinary Wild Ride. *60 Minutes – CBS News*, May 2 and August 6.

De Bono, E. 1985. *6 Thinking Hats*. Boston, MA: Little, Brown & Co.

De La Mare, N. 2009. Teaching Craft in a Designed World. September 22. Retrieved from http://creativity-online.com/news/teaching-craft-in-a-designed-world/html.

Dirlewanger, A. (no date). Open Innovation laehmt die Kreativitaet. Retrieved from www.managerseminare.de/SpeakersCorner.

Edutopia. 2010. 10 Takeaway Tips for Project-Based Learning. Retrieved from www.edutopia.org.

Epstein, A. 2010. *The Corporate Creative. Tips and Tactics for Thriving as an In-House Designer*. Cincinnati, OH: HOW Books.

Gelb, M. 1998. *How to Think Like Leonardo da Vinci*. New York, NY: Random House.

General, S. & Lantelme, G. 2010. Von der Idee zum Spin-Off – Nutzen von Kreativitaets-workshops zur Entwicklung und Umsetzung von Geschaeftsideen. In P. Harland & M. Schwarz-Geschka (Eds.), (515–527), op.cit.

Geschka & Partner Unternehmensberatung (undated). Company Information Brochure.

Geschka, H. & Zirm, A. 2005. Kreativitaetstechniken. In S. Albers and O. Gassman (Hrsg.), *Handbuch Technologie- und Innovationsmanagement*. Wiesbaden, Germany: Gabler Verlag.

Gesellschaft fuer Kreativitaet. (n.d.). 12 Thesen der Gesellschaft fuer Kreativitaet. Retrieved from www.kreativ-sein.org.

Gregory, Danny. 2006. *The Creative License*. New York, NY: Hyperion.

Harland, P. & Schwarz-Geschka, M. (Eds.). 2010. Immer eine Idee Voraus: Wie innovative Unternehmen Kreativitaet systematisch nutzen. Lichtenberg (Odw.). Germany: Harland Media.

Harrison, Sam. 2010. Creativity: Present a Powerful Pitch. Retrieved from www.howdesign.com.

DOI: 10.1057/9781137531223.0011

Hirshberg, J. 1998. *The Creative Priority – Driving Innovative Business in the Real World.* New York, NY: Harper Business.

Inc. Staff. 2010. How to Hire for Creativity. *Inc.* Guidebook, 2(6).

Isaksen, S. 2010. A System's View of Creativity: Searching for the Whole Elephant. In P. Harland & M. Schwarz-Geschka (Eds.), (21–30), op.cit.

Lehnen-Beyel, I. 2004. Macht nur Fleiss das Genie zum Genie? *SPIEGEL Online Wissenschaft.* Dezember 18. Retrieved from www.spiegel.de/ wissenschaft/mensch.

Martin, R. 2011. The Innovation Catalyst – The Best Creative Thinking Happens on a Company's Front Lines. You Just Need to Encourage It. *Harvard Business Review,* June 83–87.

McMeekin's, G. 2000. *The 12 Secrets of Highly Creative Women: A Portable Mentor.* Emeryville, CA: MJF Books.

Meyer, P. 2000. *Quantum Creativity.* Lincolnwood (Chicago), IL: Contemporary Books.

Michalko, M. 2001. *Cracking Creativity: The Secrets of Creative Genius.* Berkeley, CA: Ten Speed Press.

Monahan, T. 2002. *The Do-It-Yourself Lobotomy: Open Your Mind to Greater Creative Thinking.* New York, NY: John Wiley & Sons, Inc.

Neumeier, M. 2009. *The Designful Company.* Berkeley, CA: New Riders.

O'Doherty, S. 2007. *Getting Unstuck without Coming Unglued. A Woman's Guide to Unblocking Creativity.* Emeryville, CA: SEAL Press.

Oldach, M. 1995. *Creativity for Graphic Designers: A Real-World Guide to Idea Generation – From Defining Your Message to Selecting the Best Idea for Your Printed Piece.* China: North Light Books.

Piirto, J. 2004. *Understanding Creativity.* Scottsdale, AZ: Great Potential Press, Inc.

Pink, D. 2009. *Drive. The Surprising Truth about What Motivates Us.* New York, NY: Riverheads Books.

Pinker, S. 2009. *How the Mind Works.* New York, NY: W. W. Norton & Company.

Rasberry, S. & Selwyn, P. 1995. *Living Your Life Out Loud: How to Unlock Your Creativity and Unleash You Joy.* New York, NY: Pocket Books.

Robinson, K, Sir. 2001. *Out of Our Minds: Learning to Be Creative.* Oxford, England: Sparks Computer Solutions.

Rusch, W. 2010. *Kreativitaet – Eine Schluesselkompetenz fuer Gegenwart und Zukunft. Vortrag im Rahmen der Bildungsmesse didacta in Koeln.* Initiative Hobby Kreativ. Retrieved from www.initiative-hobbykreativ.de/kreativitaetsfoerderung3.html.

DOI: 10.1057/9781137531223.0011

SARK. 1999. *A Creative Companion. How to Free Your Creative Spirit.* Berkeley, CA: Celestial Arts.

Segal, M. 2000. *Creativity and Personality Type: Tools for Understanding and Inspiring the Many Voices of Creativity.* Huntington Beach, CA: Telos Publications.

Silverstein, M. & Sayre, K. 2009. The Female Economy. *Harvard Business Review*, September: 46–53.

Singh, V., Walther, B., Wood, K. & Jensen, D. 2009. Innovation through tRaNsFoRmAtIoNaL Design. In A. Markman & K. Wood (Eds.), *Tools for Innovation*, (171–194). Oxford, England: Oxford University Press.

Specht, Guenter. 2010. Kompetenz and Prozessorientierung im Ideenmanagement. In P. Harland and M. Schwarz-Geschka (Eds.), (451–478), op.cit.

Stauffer, D. 2005. *Thinking Clockwise: A Field Guide for the Innovative Leaders.* Minneapolis, MN: MinneApple Press.

Summers, J., Anandan, S. & Teegavarapu, S. 2009. Introduction of Design Enabling Tools: Development, Validation and Lessons Learned. In A. Markman & K. Wood (Eds.), (195–215), op.cit.

Thagard, P. 2010. How to Be Creative. *Psychology Today*, May 28. Retrieved from www.psychologytoday.com.

Tharpe, T. 2003. *The Creative Habit: Learn It and Use It for Life.* New York, NY: Simon and Schuster.

Thompson, N. 2002. May the Source Be with You. *The Washington Monthly*, 34(7–8): 34–36.

Tversky, B. & Suwa, M. 2009. Thinking with Sketches. In A. Markman & K. Wood (Eds.), (75–84), op.cit.

Vaske, H. 1999. *Why Are you Creative?* Mainz, Germany: Verlag Hermann Schmidt.

Von Cube, F. 2011. Lust an Leistung. *Ideenmanagement: Zeitschrift fuer Vorschlagswesen und Verbesserungsprozesse*, 2 (Quartal): 39–40.

Von Fange, E. 1959. *Professional Creativity.* Englewood Cliffs, NJ: Prentice Hall Inc.

Von Oech, R. 1990. *A Whack on the Side of the Head: How You Can Be More Creative.* Stamford, CT: U.S. Games Systems, Inc.

Weisberg, R. 2009. On "Out-of-the-Box" Thinking in Creativity. In A. Markman and K. Wood (Eds.), (23–47), op.cit.

Williams, T. S. 2002. *Creative Utopia. 12 Ways to Realize Total Creativity.* Cincinnati, OH: How Design Books.

DOI: 10.1057/9781137531223.0011

Bibliography

Abele, J. (2011). Bringing Minds Together – The Founder of Boston Scientific – Which Is Renowned for Its Collaborative Processes – Explains How It Really Happens. *Harvard Business Review*, July–August, 86–93.

Abercrombie, N. (2004). *Sociology.* Cambridge, England: Polity Press Ltd.

Adler, P., Heckscher, C., & Prusak. L. (2011). Building a Collaborative Enterprise: Four Keys to Creating a Culture of Trust and Teamwork. *Harvard Business Review*, July–August, 95–101.

Adolf, M., Mast, J., & Stehr, N. (2013). The Foundations of Innovation in Modern Societies: The Displacement of Concepts and Knowledgeability. *Mind and Society, Cognitive Studies in Economics and Social Sciences*, February 12. Retrieved from http://www.researchgate. net/publication/257677364_The_foundations_of_ innovation_in_modern_societies_the_displacement_ of_concepts_and_knowledgeability_2013.

Albert, R. & Runco, M. (1999). A History of Creativity. In R. Sternberg (Ed.), (16–21), op.cit.

Aleinikov, A., Kackmeister, S., & Koenig, R. (2000). *Creating Creativity: 101 Definitions (What Webster Never Told You).* Midland, Michigan: Alden B. Dow Creativity Center Press.

Alexander, V. (2003). *Sociology of the Arts: Exploring Fine and Popular Forms.* London, England: Blackwell Publishing.

Amabile, T. (1982). Social Psychology of Creativity: A Consensual Assessment Technique. *Journal of Personality and Social Psychology*, 43(5), 997–1013.

Amabile, T. (1983a). *The Social Psychology of Creativity*. New York, NY: Springer Verlag.

Amabile, T. (1983b). The Social Psychology of Creativity: A Componential Conceptualization. *Journal of Personality and Social Psychology, 45*(2), 357–376.

Amabile, T., Conti, R., Coon, H., Lazenby, J., & Michael Herron, M. (1996). Assessing the Work Environment for Creativity. *Academy of Management Journal, 39*(5), 1154–1184.

Amabile, T. & N. Gryskiewicz. (1989). The Creative Environment Scales: Work Environment Inventory. *Creativity Research Journal, 2*, 231–253.

Amabile, T. & Pillemer, J. (2012). Perspectives on the Social Psychology of Creativity. *The Journal of Creative Behavior, 46*(March, 1), 3–15.

American Academy of Arts and Sciences. (2013). The Heart of the Matter. The Humanities and Social Sciences for a Vibrant, Competitive, and Secure Nation (Report Brief). Cambridge, MA: American Academy of Arts and Sciences. Retrieved from http://www.humanitiescommission.org/_pdf/hss_report.pdf.

American Education. (n.d.). HR's Workplace Learning and Development Team, the AU Innovation Facilitators, and the Center for Teaching, Research and Learning. Retrieved from http://search.american.edu/search?q=cache:6lbN4n8wWV4J:www.american.edu/training/Profdev/upload/April-6-Quotes-on-Creativity.

Andreasen, N. (2014). Secrets of the Creative Brain. *The Atlantic*, July–August. Retrieved from http://www.theatlantic.com/features/archive/2014/06/secrets-of-the-creative-brain/372299/.

Andersson, Å. & Sahlin, N-E. (1997). *The Complexity of Creativity*. London, England: Kluwer Academic Publishers.

Antonietti, A. & Cornoldi, C. (2006). Creativity in Italy. In J. Kaufman & R. Sternberg (Eds.), (124–166), op.cit.

Armstrong, T. (1999). *7 Kinds of Smart: Identifying and Developing Your Multiple Intelligences*. New York, NY: Plume Book.

Babbie, E. (2010). *The Practice of Social Research*. Belmont, CA: Wadsworth.

Baer, J. (2012). Domain Specificity and the Limits of Creativity Theory. *The Journal of Creative Behavior, 46*(March, 1), 16–29.

Baer, J. & Kaufman, J. (2006). Creativity Research in English-Speaking Countries. In J. Kaufman & R. Sternberg (Eds.), (10–38), op.cit.

Baerveldt, C. & Cresswell, J. (2015). Creativity and the Generative Approach to Culture and Meaning. In V. P. Glăveanu, A. Gillespie, & J. Valsiner (Eds.), (93–109), op.cit.

DOI: 10.1057/9781137531223.0012

Barnard College, Columbia University. (2010). *A Conference on the Philosophy of Creativity*, October 28–30.

Bartlett, T. (2014). Madness and the Muse: We're Captivated by the Idea of the Troubled Genius. But Is It Fiction? in *The Chronicle of Higher Education, The Chronicle Review*. Retrieved from http://chronicle.com/article/Madnessthe-Muse/148845/.

Becker, G. (2008). The Alleged Connection between Creativity and Psychopathology: A Sociological Critique. Paper presented at the annual meeting of the American Sociological Association, Boston, MA, July 31. Retrieved from http://www.allacademic.com/one/www.index.

Becker, H. (1974). Art as Collective Action. *American Sociological Review*, 39(December, 6), 767–776.

Becker, H. (1982). *Art Worlds*. Berkeley, CA: University of California Press.

Benokraitis, N. (2012). *Soc*. Belmont, CA: Wadsworth.

Berger, P. & Luckmann, T. (1967). *The Social Construction of Reality: A Treatise in the Sociology of Knowledge*. New York, NY: Anchor Books.

Bergin, T. G. & Fisch, M. H. (transl.). (1968). *The New Science of Giambattista Vico*. Ithaca, NY: Cornell University Press (Original work published 1744).

Bett, W. R. (1952). *The Infirmities of Genius*. New York, NY: Philosophical Library.

Bijker, W., Hughes, T., & Pinch, T. (1987). *The Social Construction of Technological Systems: New Directions in the Sociology and History of Technology*. Cambridge, MA: MIT Press.

Black, R. (1995). *Broken Crayons: Break Your Crayons and Draw Outside the Lines*. Athens, GA: Cre8ng Places Press.

Boslough, J. (1990). The Enigma of Time. *National Geographic*, March, 109–132.

Bourdieu, P. (1979). *Distinction: A Social Critique of the Judgment of Taste*. London, England: Routledge.

Breton, P. (2007). Between Science and Rhetoric: A Recurrent Debate on the Role of Communication and Creativity in the Definition of Knowledge. In A. Sales & M. Fournier (Eds.), (115–128), op.cit.

Bridewell, W., Borrett, S., & Langley, P. (2009). Supporting Innovative Construction of Explanatory Scientific Models. In A. Markman & K. Wood (Eds.), (216–234), op.cit.

Brodbeck, K-H. (2006). Neue Trends in der Kreativitaets-Forschung. *Psychologie in Österreich*, 4&5, 246–253.

DOI: 10.1057/9781137531223.0012

Bronson, P. & Merryman, A. (2010). The Creativity Crisis – For the First Time, Research Shows that American Creativity Is Declining. What Went Wrong – And How We Can Fix It, in *Newsweek* Special Edition: The Science of Innovation and How to Reignite Our Imaginations, July 19, 44–50.

Brooks, D. (2000). *Bobos in Paradise: The New Upper Class and How They Got There.* New York, NY: Simon and Schuster.

Brown, T. (2009). *Change by Design: How Design Thinking Transforms Organizations and Inspires Innovations.* New York, NY: Harper Collins Publishers.

Brown, T. & Wyatt, J. (2007). Design Thinking for Social Innovation. *Stanford Social Innovation Review*, Stanford Graduate School of Business.

Calhoun, C. (2007). Information Technology and the International Public Sphere. In A. Sales & M. Fournier (Eds.), (77–96), op.cit.

Catmull, E. (2008). How Pixar Fosters Collective Creativity. *Harvard Business Review*, September, 64–72.

Cattell, R. B. (1963). Theory of Fluid and Crystallized Intelligence: A Critical Experiment. *Journal of Educational Psychology*, 54, 1–22.

Chambers, V. (2001). The Joy of Doing Things Badly. *The O Magazine*, November, 219.

CHI Conference. (2009). Creativity Challenges and Opportunities in Social Computing. Boston, MA, April 4–9.

Choe, I-S. (2006). Creativity – A Sudden Rising Star in Korea. In J. Kaufman & R. Sternberg (Eds.), (395–420), op.cit.

Christensen, B. T. & Schunn, C. (2009). Putting Blinkers on a Blind Man: Providing Cognitive Support for Creative Processes with Environmental Cues. In A. Markman & K. Wood (Eds.), (48–74), op.cit.

Clark, T. N. (2002). Urban Amenities: Lakes, Opera, and Juice Bars. Do They Drive Development? The City as an Entertainment Machine. *Research in Urban Policy*, Vol. 9. New York, NY: JAI Press/Elsevier.

Collins, R. (1997). The Creativity of Intellectual Networks and the Struggle over Attention Space. In A. Sales & M. Fournier (Eds.), (156–165), op.cit.

Collins, R. (1998). *The Sociology of Philosophies: A Global Theory of Intellectual Change.* Cambridge, MA: The Belknap Press of Harvard University Press.

Commission of the European Communities. (2007). *Communication from the Commission to the European Parliament, the Council, the*

European Economic and Social Committee and the Committee of the Regions – On a European Agenda for Culture in a Globalizing World (SEC(2007)570), Brussels, October 10.

Cowen, T. (2011). *The Great Stagnation: How America Ate All the Low-Hanging Fruit of Modern History, Got Sick, and Will (Eventually) Feel Better.* New York, NY: Dutton.

Cowen, T. (2013). *Average Is Over. Powering America beyond the Age of the Great Stagnation.* New York, NY: Dutton.

Crawford, M. (2009a). After Acquiring a Ph.D. and an Information-Age Resume, I Opened a Motorcycle-Repair Shop. And That's Where I Learned to Think. The Case for Working with Your Hands. *New York Times Magazine,* May 24.

Crawford, M. (2009b). *Shop Class as Soulcraft: An Inquiry into the Value of Work.* New York, NY: The Penguin Press.

Cropley, A. (1997a). Creativity and Mental Health in Everyday Life. In M. Runco & R. Richards (Eds.), *Eminent Creativity, Everyday Creativity, and Health.* Stamford, CT: Ablex Publishing Corporation, 231–246.

Cropley, A. (1997b). Fostering Creativity in the Classroom: General Principles. In M. Runco (Ed.), (83–114), op.cit.

Cropley, A. (1999a). Definitions of Creativity. In M. Runco and S. Pritzker (Eds.), *Encyclopedia of Creativity,* Vol. 1 (A–H), (511–524). San Diego, CA: Academic Press.

Cropley, A. (1999b). Education. In M. Runco and S. Pritzker (Eds.), *Encyclopedia of Creativity,* Vol. 1 (A–H), (629–642). San Diego, CA: Academic Press.

Cropley, A. (2009). *Creativity in Education and Learning: A Guide for Teachers and Educators.* New York, NY: RoutledgeFalmer.

Csikszentmihalyi, M. (1996). *Creativity: Flow and the Psychology of Discovery and Invention.* New York, NY: Harper Collins Publishers

Csikszentmihalyi, M. (1998). Society, Culture and Person, a Systems View of Creativity. In R. Sternberg (Ed.), *The nature of creativity: Contemporary Psychological Perspectives.* Cambridge, England: Cambridge University Press, 325–339.

Csikszentmihalyi, M. (1999). Implications of a Systems Perspective for the Study of Creativity. In R. Sternberg (Ed.), (313–338), op.cit.

Csikszentmihalyi, M. (2003). Key Issues in Creativity and Development, Prepared by All Authors. In R. K. Sawyer et al. (Eds.), 217–233, op.cit.

DOI: 10.1057/9781137531223.0012

Cunliffe, L. (2009). *The Problem with Assessment in Art and Design Education.* Keynote Speaker, Measuring Unique Studies Effectively (MUSE) Conference, February 8–11, Savannah, Georgia.

Cusack, J. (1994). Book Review of R. Finke, T. Ward, and S. Smith. Creative Cognition: Theory, Research, and Application. Cambridge, MA, MIT Press in *American Journal of Psychiatry*, 151(May, 5), 777.

De Bono, E. (1985). *6 Thinking Hats.* Boston, MA: Little, Brown and Co.

Designboom. (n.d.). Biomimicry. Retrieved from http://www.designboom.com/contemporary/biomimicry.html.

Discovery Channel. (n.d.). *Through the Wormhole.* Retrieved from http://science.discovery.com/tv-shows/through-the-wormhole/videos/creativity-cap.html.

DuPont Employees. (1990). *Are We Creative Yet?* With cartoons by Bob Thaves. The DuPont Company, ACA Press.

The Economist Technology Quarterly. (2009). Father of the Cell Phone, June, 30–32.

Eisenman, R. (1997b). Mental Illness, Deviance, and Creativity. In M. Runco, *The Creativity Research Handbook*, Vol. 1. (295–312). Cresskill, NJ: Hampton Press.

Ekvall, G. (1993). Creativity in Project Work: A Longitudinal Study of a Product Development Project. *Creativity in Project Work*, 2(1), 17–26.

Ekvall, G. (1996). Organizational Climate for Creativity and Innovation. *European Journal of Work and Organizational Psychology,* 5(1), 105–123.

Ekvall, G. (1997). Organizational Conditions and Levels of Creativity. *Creativity and Innovation Management*, 6(4), 195–205.

Ekvall, G. (1999). Creative Climate. In M. Runco & S. Pritzker (Eds.), *Encyclopedia of Creativity*, Vol. 1 (A–H), (403–412). San Diego, CA: Academic Press.

Ekvall, G. (2000). Management and Organizational Philosophies and Practices as Stimulants or Blocks to Creative Behavior: A Study of Engineers. *Creativity and Innovation Management*, 9(2), 94–99.

Ellis, H. 2009. *A Study of British Genius.* New York, NY: Cornell University Library (originally published 1904).

Emanuel, R. (2013). A Time for Renewal: America's Infrastructure Is in a Dire State, Stimulating a Search for Creative Solutions. *The Economist*, March 16. Special Report: America's Competitiveness.

English, M. (2011). Creativity Not as Well Receive as We Think. *Psychology,* August 31. Retrieved from http://news.discovery.com/human/psychology/creativity-110831.htm.

Epstein, A. (2010). *The Corporate Creative: Tips and Tactics for Thriving as an In-House Designer.* Cincinnati, OH: HOW Books.

Esquivel, G. & Peters, K. (1999). Diversity, Cultural. In M. Runco & S. Pritzker (Eds.), *Encyclopedia of Creativity*, Vol. 1 (A–H), (583–589). San Diego, CA: Academic Press.

European Commission, Joint Research Centre, Institute for the Protection and Security of the Citizen. (2009a). *CRELL (Centre for Research on Lifelong Learning) International Conference: Can Creativity Be Measured?* May 28–29, Brussels. Retrieved from http://crell.jrc. ec.europa.eu/creativitydebate/.

European Commission. (2009b). *European Year of Creativity.* Retrieved from http://create2009.europa.eu.

Everett, D. (2008). *Don't Sleep. There Are Snakes. Life and Language in the Amazonian Jungle.* New York, NY: Vintage Departures/Vintage Books.

Everett, D. (2012). *Language. The Cultural Tool.* New York, NY: Pantheon Books.

Eysenck, H. (1997). Creativity and Personality: Word Association, Origence and Psychoticism. In M. Runco and R. Richards (Eds.), *Eminent Creativity, Everyday Creativity, and Health*, (107–118), Geenwich, CT: Ablex Publishing Co.

Fayard, A-L. & Weeks, J. (2011). Who Moved My Cube? Creating Workspaces that Actually Foster Collaboration. *Harvard Business Review*, July–August, 103–110.

Feinstein, J. (2006). *The Nature of Creative Development.* Stanford, CA: Stanford Business Books.

Feldman, D. H. (1999). The Development of Creativity. In R. Sternberg (Ed.), (169–188), op.cit.

Feldman, D. H. & Gardner, H. (2003). The Creation of Multiple Intelligences Theory. A Study in High-Level Thinking. In R. K. Sawyer et al. (Eds.), (139–185), op.cit.

Fischer, G. (2011). Social Creativity: Exploiting the Power of Cultures of Participation. Keynote Address of the 7th International Conference on Semantics, Knowledge and Grids, China.

Fischer, G. (2013). Learning, Social Creativity, and Cultures of Participation. Retrieved from http://genius.com/Gerhard-fischer-learning-social-creativity-and-cultures-of-participation-annotated.

Fischer, K. (2013). The Employment Mismatch: A College Degree Sorts Job Applicants, but Employers Wish It Meant More. Special Reports.

DOI: 10.1057/9781137531223.0012

The Chronicle of Higher Education, 3/6. Retrieved from http://chronicle. com/article/The-Employment-Mismatch/137625/#id=overview.

Fisher, C., Busch-Rossnagel, N., Jopp, D., & Brown, J. (2012). Applied Developmental Science, Social Justice, and Socio-Political Well-Being. *Applied Developmental Science,* 16(1), 54–64.

Fisher, C. & Lerner, R. (2013). Promoting Positive Development through Social Justice: An Introduction to a New Ongoing Section of *Applied Developmental Science. Applied Developmental Science,* 17(2), 57–59.

Flora, C. (2009). Everyday Creativity, Everyday Genius. *Psychology Today,* November–December. Retrieved from https://www. psychologytoday.com/articles/200910/everyday-creativity.

Florida, R. (2002). *The Rise of the Creative Class; and How It's Transforming Work, Leisure, Community, and Everyday Life.* New York, NY: Basic Books.

Forbes, P. (2005). *The Gecko's Foot. Bio-inspiration: Engineering New Materials from Nature.* New York, NY: W. W. Norton & Company.

Fox, M. (2004). *Creativity – Where the Divine and the Human Meet.* NY: Jeremy P. Tarcher, Penguin.

Fox, N. (2013). Creativity, Anti-humanism, and the "New Sociology of Art." *Journal of Sociology,* August 28. Retrieved from http://jos. sagepub.com/content/early/2013/08/27/1440783313498947.

The Free Dictionary. (1979). Creativity. Retrieved from http:// encyclopedia2.thefreedictionary.com/creativity.

Fuller, S. (2007). Creativity in an Orwellian Key: A Sceptic's Guide to the Post-Sociological Imaginary. In A. Sales & M. Fournier (Eds.), (97–114), op.cit.

Galenson, D. (2004a). The Life Cycles of Modern Artists. *Historical Methods,* 37(3), 123–136.

Galenson, D. (2004b). A Portrait of the Artist as Young or Old Innovators: The Creative Life Cycle of Modern Poets and Novelists. *World Economics,* 5(4), 175.

Galenson, D. (2006). Age + Creativity: During What Portion of Their Lives Are Great Innovators Most Creative? *The Milken Institute Review,* Second Quarter, 28–37.

Galenson, D. (2009). Understanding Creativity. Paper prepared for the Center for Creativity Economics, Universidad del CEMA, Buenos Aires.

Galindo, J. (2010). Creative Ideas in a Flash: 5 Principles for Harnesssing Group Creativity for Ideation. Retrieved from http://www.

DOI: 10.1057/9781137531223.0012

picklesanddoughnuts.com/creative-ideas-in-a-flash-5-principles-for-harnessing-group-creativity-for-ideation/.

Galton, F. (1869). *Hereditary Genius*. Biblio. Life, LLC Reproduction.

Garber, M. (2002). Our Genius Problem. *Atlantic Monthly*, 5, December.

Gardner, H. (1983). *Frames of Mind: The Theory of Multiple Intelligences*. New York, NY: Basic Books.

Gardner, H. (1993). *Creative Minds: An Anatomy of Creativity Seen through the Lives of Freud, Einstein, Picasso, Stravinsky, Eliot, Graham and Gandhi*. New York, NY: Basic Books.

Gavetti, G. (2011). The New Psychology of Strategic Leadership: Cognitive Science Sheds Fresh Light on What It Takes to Be Innovative. *Harvard Business Review*, July–August, 118–125.

Geer, C. (2011a). Innovation 101. Anybody Can Be Creative, Says David Kelley. You Just Have to Learn How. *The Wall Street Journal*, October 17.

Geer, C. (2011b). How to Innovate More? Practice. Practice. Practice. *Business Technology,* October 17. Retrieved from http://www.wsj.com/articles/SB10001424052970204831304576596714181439514.

Genovard, C., Prieto, M. D., Bermejo, M. R., & Fernandiz, C. (2006). History of Creativity in Spain. In J. Kaufman and R. Sternberg (Eds.), (68–95), op.cit.

GEO Wissen. (1993). Chaos + Kreativitaet, Nachdruck. November.

Gergen, K. (2010). *An Invitation to Social Construction*. (2nd ed.). Thousand Oaks, CA: SAGE Publications.

Giddens, A. (1982). *Sociology: A Brief but Critical Introduction*. London, England: Macmillan.

Gillespie, A., Baerveldt, C., Costall, A., Cresswell, J., De Saint-Laurent, C., Glăveanu, V. P., John-Steiner, V., Jovchelovitch, S., Sawyer, R. K., Tanggaard, L., Valsiner, J., Wagoner, B., & Zittoun, T. (2015). Discussing Creativity from a Cultural Psychological Perspective. In V. P. Glăveanu et al. (Eds.), (125–140), op.cit.

Gimmler, A. (2006). Creative Pragmatism and the Social Sciences, a Discussion between Hans Joas and Richard Sennett, Moderated by Antje Gimmler. *Distinktion*, 13, 5–31.

Gladwell, M. (2002a). Group Think. *The New Yorker,* December 2. Retrieved from http://www.newyorker.com/magazine/2002/12/02/group-think.

Gladwell, M. (2002b). *The Tipping Point – How Little Things Can Make a Big Difference*. New York, NY: Little, Brown and Company.

DOI: 10.1057/9781137531223.0012

Glass, N. & Knight, M. (2013). How Humble USB Turned Engineer into Tech "Rock Star." April 26. Retrieved from http://www.cnn.com/2013/04/26/tech/innovation/usb-intel-billion-seller/index.html.

Glăveanu, V. P. (2010). Principles for a Cultural Psychology of Creativity. *Culture & Psychology*, 16(2), 147–163.

Glăveanu, V. P. (2011a). Children and Creativity: A Most (un)Likely Pair? *Thinking Skills and Creativity*, 6, 122–131.

Glăveanu, V. P. (2011b). Creating Creativity: Reflections from Fieldwork. *Integrative Psychological and Behavioral Science*, 45(March, 1), 100–115.

Glăveanu, V. P. (2011c). How Are We Creative Together?: Comparing Sociocognitive and Sociocultural Answers. *Theory and Psychology*, 21(4), 473–492.

Glăveanu, V. P. (2013). Habitual Creativity: Revising Habit, Reconceptualizing Creativity. *Review of General Psychology*, 16(March, 1), 78–92.

Glăveanu, V. P. (2014a). *Distributed Creativity: Thinking Outside the Box of the Creative Individual*. New York, NY: Springer Briefs in Psychology.

Glăveanu, V. P. (2014b). *Thinking through Creativity and Culture: Toward an Integrated Model*. History and Theory of Psychology. Piscataway, NJ: Transaction Publishers.

Glăveanu, V. P. & Gillespie, A. (2015). Creativity Out of Difference: Theorising the Semiotic, Social and Temporal Origin of Creative Acts. In V. P. Glăveanu, A. Gillespie, & J. Valsiner, (1–15), op.cit.

Glăveanu, V. P., Gillespie, A., & Valsiner, J. (2014). *Rethinking Creativity: Contributions from Social and Cultural Psychology (Cultural Dynamics of Social Representation)*. London, England: Routledge.

Goldstein, E. (2010). How College Kills Creativity. *The Chronicle Review*, B16, November 26.

Göttlich, U. (2012). Medienaneignung und symbolische Kreativitaet. In U. Göttlich and R. Kurt (Eds.), (133–148), op.cit.

Göttlich, U. & Kurt, R. (Hrsg). (2012). *Kreativitaet und Improvisation. Soziologische Positionen*. Wiesbaden, Germany: Springer.

Grant, A. M. & Berry, J. W. (2011). The Necessity of Others Is the Mother of Invention: Intrinsic and Prosocial Motivations, Perspective Taking, and Creativity. *Academy of Management Journal*, 54(1), 73–96.

Grossman, L. (2011). Reinventing the Inventor – In the Age of Steve Jobs, It's All about Perfecting the Final Product. Nobody Remembers the Guy Who Had the Idea in the First Place, (56–86), *Time* Magazine, Special Double Issue, November 28.

DOI: 10.1057/9781137531223.0012

Grütters, M. (2015). Rede von Kulturstaatsministerin Monika Grütters bei der Veranstaltung der Deutschen Content Allianz, "Kreativität in der digitalen Welt." *Die Bundesregierung,* February 24. Retrieved from http://www.bundesregierung.de/Content/DE/Rede/2015/02/2015-02-25-gruetters-content-allianz.html.

Guilford, J. P. (1950). Creativity. *The American Psychologist,* 5, 444–454.

Hacking, I. (1999). *The Social Construction of What?* Cambridge, MA: Harvard University Press.

Hage, J. (1999). Organizational Innovation and Organizational Change. *Annual Review of Sociology,* 25, 597–622.

Hage, J. (2007). Knowledge and Societal Change: Institutional Coordination and the Evolution of Organizational Populations. In A. Sales & M. Fournier (Eds.), (43–66), op.cit.

Hall, R. (1987). *Organizations. Structures, Processes, and Outcomes.* (4th ed.). Englewood Cliffs, NJ: Prentice-Hall Inc.

Hargadon, A. (2004). Bridging Old Worlds and Building New Ones: Towards a Microsociology of Creativity. *Research Gate.* Retrieved from http://www.researchgate.net/publication/253734313_BRIDGING_OLD_WORLDS_AND_BUILDING_NEW_ONES_TOWARDS_A_MICROSOCIOLOGY_OF_CREATIVITY.

Harland, P. & Schwarz-Geschka, M. (Hrsg.) (2010). *Immer eine Idee Voraus: Wie innovative Unternehmen Kreativitaet systematisch nutzen.* Lichtenberg (Odw.): Harland Media.

Harrison, S. (2010). Creativity: Present a Powerful Pitch. In *Howdesign,* (82–85). Retrieved from www.howdesign.com.

Haviland, W., Prins, H., McBride, B., & Walgrath, D. (2011). *Cultural Anthropology: The Human Challenge.* (13th ed.). Belmont, CA: Wadsworth/Cengage Learning.

HBO. (2013). *The Newsroom the Complete First Season.* Burbank, CA: Home Box Office Entertainment, Inc.

Hempel, P. & Sue-Chan, C. (2010). Culture and the Assessment of Creativity. *Management and Organization Review,* 6(November 3), 415–435.

Hirshberg, J. (1998). *The Creative Priority – Driving Innovative Business in the Real World.* New York, NY: Harper Business.

HOK. (n.d.). A New Community Rooted in Nature – Lavasa Hill Station Master Plan, Mose Valley, Pune, India. The Emerging Science of Biomimicry Is Guiding the Development of Lavasa, a New Indian Hill Town Spread across 12,500 Acres of Picturesque Land Southeast

DOI: 10.1057/9781137531223.0012

of Mumbai. Retrieved from http://www.hok.com/about/sustainability/lavasa-hill-station-master-plan/.

Hollingsworth, J. (2007). High Cognitive Complexity and the Making of Major Scientific Discoveries. In A. Sales & M. Fournier (Eds.), (129–155), op.cit.

Holm-Hadulla, R., Roussel, M., & Hofmann, F-H. (2010). Drepression and Creativity – The Case of the German Poet, Scientist and Statesman J. W. von Goethe. *Journal of Affective Disorders,* 121(1–3), 43–49.

Howkins, J. (2001). *The Creative Economy.* New York, NY: Penguin Books.

Ibarra, H. & Hansen, M. (2011). Are You a Collaborative Leader? How Great CEOs Keep Their Teams Connected. *Harvard Business Review,* July–August, 69–74.

IBM. (2010). *IBM 2010 Global CEO Study: Creativity Selected as Most Crucial Factor for Future Success.* Retrieved from http://www-03.ibm.com/press/us/en/pressrelease/31670.wss.

Inc. Guidebook. (2010). *How to Hire for Creativity,* 2(6).

Isaksen, S. (2008). *A Compendium of Evidence for Creative Problem Solving.* The Creative Problem Solving Group. Sarasota, FL.

Jahnke, I., Haertel, T., & Winkler, M. (2011). Sechs Facetten der Kreativitätsförderung in der Lehre – empirische Erkentnisse. In S. Nickel (Ed.), (138–166), op.cit.

Jana, R. (2008). In Short. *Business Week,* September.

Jefferson, M. (2001). Creativity. *The O Magazine,* November, 211–212.

Joas, H. (1996). *Die Kreativitaet des Handelns.* Berlin, Germany: Suhrkamp Taschenbuch Verlag.

John-Steiner, Vera. (2014). Creative Engagement across the Lifespan. In V. P. Glăveanu, A. Gillespie & J. Valsiner (Eds.), (31–44), op.cit.

Jovchelovitch, S. (2014). The Creativity of the Social: Imagination, Development and Social Change in Rio de Janeiro's Favelas. In V. P. Glăveanu, A. Gillespie, & J. Valsiner (Eds.), (76–92), op.cit.

Karpova, E., Marcketti, S., & Barker, J. (2011). The Efficacy of Teaching Creativity: Assessment of Student Creative Thinking before and after Exercises. *Clothing & Textiles Research Journal,* 29(1), 52–66.

Kasof, J. (1999). Attribution and Creativity. In M. Runco and S. Pritzker (Eds.), *Encyclopedia of Creativity,* Vol. 1 (A–H), (147–156). San Diego, CA: Academic Press.

DOI: 10.1057/9781137531223.0012

Kaufman, J. & Sternberg, R. (2006). *The International Handbook of Creativity*, NY: Cambridge University Press.

Kelley, T. with Littman, J. (2001). *The Art of Innovation. Lessons in Creativity from IDEO, America's Leading Design Firm.* New York, NY: A Currency Book, published by Doubleday.

Kelley, T. with Littman, J. (2005). *The Ten Faces of Innovation: IDEO's Strategies for Beating the Devil's Advocate & Driving Creativity throughout Your Organization.* New York, NY: Currency Doubleday.

Kelley, T. & Kelley, D. (2013). *Creative Confidence. Unleashing the Creative Potential in All of Us.* New York, NY: Crown Business.

Kersting, K. (2003). What Exactly Is Creativity? *American Psychological Association*, November, 3410, 40. Retrieved from http://www.apa.org/monitor/nov03/creativity.aspx.

Keynes, M. (1995). Creativity and Psychopathology: A Study of 291 World-Famous Men. *British Journal of Psychiatry*, 165, 22–34.

Kim, K. H. (2007). Exploring the Interactions between Asian Culture (Confucianism) and Creativity. *The Journal of Creative Behavior*, 41(March, 1), 28–53.

Kirkpatrick, M. & Mortimer, J. (2011). Origins and Outcomes of Judgment about Work. *Social Forces*, 89(4), 1239–1260.

Kirton, M. (2003). *Adaption-Innovation in the Context of Diversity and Change.* New York, NY: Routledge.

Kirton, M. (2010). Kirton KAI Inventory Tool. Retrieved from http://pubs.acs.org/subscribe/archive/ci/31/i11/html/11hipple_box3.ci.html.

Klausen, S. (2010). The Notion of Creativity Revisited: A Philosophical Perspective on Creativity Research. *Creativity Research Journal*, 22(4), 347–360.

Kohlberg, L. (1981). *Philosophy of Moral Development: Moral Stages and the Idea of Justice. Essays on Moral Development*, Vol. 1. San Francisco, CA: Harper & Row.

Kotkin, J. (2013). Richard Florida Concedes the Limits of the Creative Class: The So-Called Creative Class of Intellects and Artists Was Supposed to Remake America's Cities and Revive Urban Wastelands. Now the Evidence Is in – and the Experiment Appears to Have Failed. *The Daily Beast*. Retrieved from http://www.thedailybeast.com/articles/2013/03/20/richard-florida-concedes-the-limits-of-the-creative-class.html.

Krämer, H. (2012). Praktiken kreativen Arbeitens in den Creative Industries. In U. Goettlich & R. Kurt (Eds.), (109–132), op.cit.

DOI: 10.1057/9781137531223.0012

Küppers, B-O. (1993). Wenn das Ganze mehr ist als die Summe seiner Teile. In *GEO Wissen, Chaos + Kreativitaet*, Nachdruck, 3/83402 (November), 28–31.

Kurt, R. & Göttlich, U. (2012). Einleitung. In U. Göttlich and R. Kurt (Eds.), (9–15), op.cit.

Kusa, D. (2007). Autonomy of Creator and Social Processes: Otherness or Positive Deviance? *Czeskoslovenska Psychologie*, 51, 80–88.

Kwasniewska, J. & Necka, E. (2004). Perception of the Climate for Creativity in the Workplace: The Role of the Level in the Organization and Gender. *Creativity and Innovation Management*, 13(3), 187–196.

LaChapelle, J. (1983). Creativity Research: Its Sociological and Educational Limitations. *JSTOR: Studies in Art Education*, 24(2), 131–139.

Langer, F. (2011). Wie es den Kindern geht? Fantastisch: Wenn kleine Forscher nach verborgenen Fakten graben, ist stets eine wundersame Macht mit im Spiel: die Fantasie. Erwachsene Wissenschaftler erkennen in ihr das wichtigste Werkzeug der Weltaneignung. Und jene Kraft, die uns zu Menschen macht. *Geo – Die Welt mit anderen Augen sehen*, July 7, 129–144.

Latour, B. (1987). *Science in Action*. Cambridge, MA: Harvard University Press.

Leavy, B. (2003). A More Creative Organization and a Better Breeding Ground for Leaders. *Irish Marketing Review*, 16(2), 51–56.

Lehrer, J. (2012). *Imagine – How Creativity Works*. Boston, MA: Houghton Mifflin Harcourt.

Lemonick, M. (1999). The Riddle of Time. *Time*, December 27, 142–144.

Lerner, R. (2013). Keynote Address at the 8th Biennial Conference of the Society for the Study of Human Development, Fort Lauderdale, FL, November 1–3.

Lindqvist, G. (2003). Vygotsky's Theory of Creativity. *Creativity Research Journal*, 15(2&3), 245–251.

Littlejohn, S. & Domenici, K. (2000). *Engaging Communication in Conflict: Systemic Practice*. Thousand Oaks, CA: Sage.

LiveScience. (2011). Why Are U.S. Children Becoming Less Creative? August 12. Retrieved from http://www.,mmm.com/ family/family-activities/stories/why-are-us-children-becoming-less-creative.

Lois, G. (2012). *Damn Good Advice (for People with Talent!) – How to Unleash Your Creative Potential by America's Master Communicator*. New York, NY: Phaidon Press Limited.

DOI: 10.1057/9781137531223.0012

Lombroso, C. (1895). *The Man of Genius*. London, England: Walter Scott, Ltd.

Lombroso, C. (1911). *The Criminal Man*. New York, NY: G.P. Putnam's Sons.

Lubart, T. (1990). Creativity and Cross-Cultural Variation. *International Journal of Psychology*, 25(1), 39–59.

Lubart, T. (1999). Creativity across Cultures. In R. Sternberg (Ed.), (339–350), op.cit.

Lubart, T. & Runco, M. (1999). Economic Perspective on Creativity. In M. Runco and S. Pritzker (Eds.), *Encyclopedia of Creativity*, Vol. 1 (A–H), (623–627). San Diego, CA: Academic Press.

Luckmann, T. (2003). Von der "Entstehung" persoenlicher Identitaet, pp. 383–390 in U. Wenzel, B. Bretzinger, & K. Holz (Eds.), *Subjekte und Gesellschaft* (383–390). Weilerswist, Germany: Velbrueck Wissenschaft.

Luckmann, T. (2004). Soziales im Kulturellen und Kulturelles im Sozialen? In J. Reichertz, A. Honer & W. Schneider (Eds.), *Hermeneutik der Kulturen – Kulturen der Hermeneutik. Zum 65. Geburtstag von Hans-Georg Soeffner* (27–40), Konstanz, Germany: UK Verlagsgesellschaft mbH.

Luckmann, T. (2008). Konstitution, Konstruktion: Phaenomenologie, Sozialwissenschaft. In J. Raab, M. Pfadenhauer, P. Stegmaier, J. Dreher and B. Schnettler (Eds.), *Phaenomenologie und Soziologie, Theoretische Positionen, aktuelle Problemfelder und empirische Umsetzungen* (33–40). Wiesbaden, Germany: VS Verlag fuer Sozialwissenschaften.

Luckmann, T. (2010). Ich habe mich nie als Konstruktivist betrachtet. In F. Herrschaft & K. Lichtblau (Eds.), *Soziologie in Frankfurt* (345–368). Wiesbaden, Germany: VS Verlag fuer Sozialwissenschaften.

Luckmann, T. (2012). Ontological Realism and the Social Construction of Reality. Opening Lecture at the International Conference on Social Construction of Reality: Chances and Risks for Human Communications, September 25–27, Yerevan State University, Armenia.

Ludwig, A. (1995). *The Price of Greatness: Resolving the Creativity and Madness Controversy*. New York, NY: Guilford Press.

Luhrmann, T. (2012). *When God Talks Back: Understanding the American Evangelical Relationship with God*. New York, NY: Vintage Book.

Macionis, J. (2009). *Society: The Basics*. (10th ed.). Upper Saddle River, NJ: Pearson/Prentice Hall.

DOI: 10.1057/9781137531223.0012

Magyari-Beck, I. (1999). Creatology. In M. Runco & S. Pritzker (Eds.), *Encyclopedia of Creativity*, Vol. 1 (A–H), (433–441). San Diego, CA: Academic Press.

Makel, M. (2009). Help Us Creativity Researchers, You're Our Only Hope. *Psychology of Aesthetics, Creativity, and the Arts*, 3(1), 38–42.

Malanga, S. (2004). The Curse of the Creative Class. Richard Florida's Theories Are All the Rage Worldwide. Trouble Is, They're Plain Wrong. Winter. Retrieved from www.city-journal.org/printable.php?id=1203.

Mandel, M. (2008). In Focus. *Business Week*, September 22.

Mangan, K. (2012). Educators, Employers, and Jobless Graduates Point Fingers at Roots of Unemployment. *The Chronicle of Higher Education, Students*, 12(12). Retrieved from http://chronicle.com/article/ Educators-Employers-and/136119/.

Markman, A. & Wood, K. (2009a). The Cognitive Science of Innovation Tools. In A. Markman & K. Wood (Eds.), (3–22), op.cit.

Markman, A. & Wood, K. (Eds.). (2009b). *Tools for Innovation*. Oxford, England: Oxford University Press.

Markman, A., Wood, K., Linsey, J., Murphy, & Laux, J. (2009). Supporting Innovation by Promoting Analogical Reasoning. In A. Markman & K. Wood (Eds.), (85–103), op.cit.

Martin, R. (2011). The Innovation Catalysts – The Best Creative Thinking Happens on a Company's Front Lines. You Just Need to Encourage It. *Harvard Business Review*, June, 2–7.

Marx, K. (1953). *Die Fruehschriften (The Economic and Philosophical Manuscripts of 1844)*. Stuttgart, Germany: Kroener.

Maslow, A. (1999). *Toward a Psychology of Being* (3rd ed.). New York, NY: John Wiley & Sons, Inc.

May, R. (1975). *The Courage to Create*. New York, NY: Bantam Books.

Mayer, R. (1999). Fifty Years of Creativity Research. In R. Sternberg (Ed.), (449–460), op.cit.

McEwan, I. (1998). *Amsterdam*. New York, NY: Anchor Books.

Merkel, A. (2006). Speech at the World Economic Forum, Davos, January 25. Retrieved from http://www.bundesregierung.de/Content/ EN/Reden/2006/01/2006-01-25-spe3ech-by-angela-merkel.

Meyer, P. (2000). *Quantum Creativity*. Lincolnwood, Chicago: Contemporary Books.

Milgram, R. & Livne, N. (2006). Research on Creativity in Israel: A Chronicle of Theoretical and Empirical Development. In J. Kaufman & R. Sternberg (Eds.), (307–336), op.cit.

DOI: 10.1057/9781137531223.0012

Miller, P. (2015). Is "Design Thinking" the New Liberal Arts? *The Chronicle of Higher Education, The Chronicle Review*, March 26. Retrieved from http://chronicle.com/article/Is-Design-Thinking-the-New/228779/.

Mills, C. W. (1951). *White Collar*. New York, NY: Oxford University Press.

Mills, C. W. (1959). *The Sociological Imagination*. London, England: Oxford University Press.

Misra, G., Srivastava, A. & Misra, I. (2006). Culture and Facets of Creativity: The Indian Experience. In J. Kaufman & R. Sternberg (Eds.), (421–455), op.cit.

Moffat, W. (2010). Creativity and Collaboration in the Small College Department. *Pedagogy: Critical Approaches to Teaching Literature, Language, Composition, and Culture*, 10(2), 283–294.

Moran, S. & John-Steiner, V. (2003). Creativity in the Making: Vygotsky's Contemporary Contribution to the Dialectic of Creativity and Development. In R. K. Sawyer, et al., (Eds.), (223–224), op.cit.

Moreau, C. & Dahl, D. (2009). Constraints and Consumer Creativity. In A. Markman & K. Wood (Eds.), (104–127), op.cit.

Morris, M. & Leung, K. (2010). Creativity East and West: Perspectives and Parallels. *Management and Organization Review*, 6(3): 313–327.

Mouchiroud, C. & Lubbart, T. (2006). Past, Present, and Future Perspective on Creativity in France and French-Speaking Switzerland. In J. Kaufman & R. Sternberg (Eds.), (96–123), op.cit.

Mpofu, E., Myambo, K., Mogaji, A., Mashego, T-A., & Khaleefa, O. (2006). African Perspectives on Creativity. In J. Kaufman & R. Sternberg (Eds.), (456–489), op.cit.

National Public Radio. 2013. *Morning Edition – Interview with British Musician and Songwriter Omar Lye-Fook*. Retrieved from http://npr.org/player/v2/mediaPlayer.html?action=1&islist=false&id=196299664&m=196513466.

Necka, E., Grohman, M., & Stabosz, A. (2006). Creativity Studies in Poland. In J. Kaufman & R. Sternberg (Eds.), (270–306), op.cit.

Neffe, J. (2008). *Darwin. Das Abenteuer des Lebens*. Muenchen, Germany: C. Bertelsmann.

Nickel, S. (2011). *Der Bologna-Prozess aus Sicht der Hochschulforschung. Analysen und Impulse für die Praxis*. Bundesministerium für Bildung und Forschung. Arbeitspaper, 148, September.

Niu, W. (2006). Development of Creativity Research in Chinese Societies: A Comparison of Mainland China, Taiwan, Hong King, and Singapore. In J. Kaufman & R. Sternberg (Eds.), (374–394), op.cit.

DOI: 10.1057/9781137531223.0012

Niu, W. & Liu, D. (2009). Enhancing Creativity: A Comparison between Effects of an Indicative Instruction "to Be Creative" and a More Elaborate Heuristic Instruction on Chinese Student Creativity. *Psychology of Aesthetics, Creativity and the Arts,* (3)2: 93–98.

Obama, B. (2011). *State of the Union Address.* Retrieved from https://www.whitehouse.gov/state-of-the-union-2011.

Oelze, B. (2012). Ideen zu einer phaenomenologischen Soziologie der Keativitaet. In U. Göttlich & R. Kurt (Eds.), (79–98), op.cit.

Oldach, Mark. (1995). *Creativity for Graphic Designers: A Real-World Guide to Idea Generation – From Defining Your Message to Selecting the Best Idea for Your Printed Piece.* China: North Light Books.

Olien, J. (2013). Inside the Box. People Don't Actually Like Creativity. *SLATE.* Retrieved from http://www.slate.com/articles/health_and_science/science/2013/12/creativity_is_rejected_teachers_and_bosses_don_t_value_out_of_the_box_thinking.html.

Oral, G. (2006). Creativity in Turkey and Turkish-Speaking Countries. In J. Kaufman & R. Sternberg (Eds.), (337–373), op.cit.

Orbach, B. Y. (2002). The Law and Economics of Creativity in the Workplace. Discussion paper No. 356, Harvard Law School, the Center for Law, Economics and Business. Retrieved from http://www.law.harvard.edu/programs/olin_center/.

Pappano, Laura. (2014). Learning to Think Outside the Box. Creativity Becomes an Academic Discipline. *New York Times Magazine,* February. Retrieved from http://nytimes.com/2014/02/09/education/edlife/creativity-becomes-an-academic-discipline.html.

Parnes, S. (2010). Herr Creativity of Germany. Welcome Note. In P. Harland & M. Schwarz-Geschka (Ed.), (xiii), op.cit.

Passoth, J-H. (2012). Heterogene Praktiken, variable Kreativitaeten. In U. Göttlich & R. Kurt (Eds.), (45–62), op.cit.

Peck, J. (2005). Struggling with the Creative Class. *International Journal of Urban and Regional Research,* 29(December, 4), 740–770.

Pettinger, L. (n.d.). *What is Creativity? A Sociological Exploration.* Retrieved from http://www.city.ac.uk/research/resdev_dps.

Pfohl, H-C. (2010). Innovationsmanagement in der Logistik. In P. Harland & M. Schwarz-Geschka (Eds.), (105–118), op.cit.

Pfütze, H. (2012). Kreativer Widerstand gegen die Event-Kultur. In U. Göttlich & R. Kurt (Eds.), (239–262), op.cit.

Pinch, T. & Bijker, W. (1984). The Social Construction of Facts and Artefacts: Or How the Sociology of Science and the Sociology of

DOI: 10.1057/9781137531223.0012

Technology Might Benefit Each Other. *Social Studies of Science,* August 14, 399–441.

Pink, D. (2010). *Drive. The Surprising Truth about What Motivates Us.* New York, NY: Riverheads Books.

Plafker, T. (2003). International Education: China Seeks Ways to Nurture Creativity. *New York Times Magazine,* October 21. Retrieved from http://www.nytimes.com/2003/10/21/news/21iht-rchina_ed3_.html.

Plato. (1992). *The Republic* (translated by G. M. A. Grube and revised by C. D. C. Reeve). Indianapolis, Cambridge: Hackett Publishing Company, Inc.

Porzio, S. (2003). A Critical Review of Eysenck's Theory of Psychoticism and How It Relates to Creativity. Retrieved from www.personalityresearch.org/papers/porzio.html.

Post, F. (1994). Creativity and Psychopathology: A Study of 291 World-Famous Men. *British Journal of Psychiatry,* 165, 22–34.

Preiser, S. (2006). Creativity Research in German-Speaking Countries. In J. Kaufman and R. Sternberg (Eds.), (167–201), op.cit.

Preiss, D. & Strasser, D. (2006). Creativity in Latin America: Views from Psychology, Humanities, and the Arts. In J. Kaufman & R. Sternberg (Eds.), (39–67), op.cit.

Preisz, J. (Hrsg.) (2010). *Jahrbuch der Kreativitaet.* Koeln, Germany: Marketing & Kommunikation.

Puccio, G., Mance, M., Switalski, L. B., & Reali, P. (2012). *Creativity Rising.* Buffalo, NY: ICSC Press.

Purser, R. & Montuori, A. (2000). In Search of Creativity: Beyond Individualism and Collectivism. Western Academy of Management Conference, Kona HI. Retrieved from http://online.sfsu.edu/~rpurser/revised/pages/CREATIVITYwam.htm.

Raina, M. K. (1999). Cross-Cultural Differences. In M. Runco & S. Pritzker (Eds.), *Encyclopedia of Creativity,* Vol. 1 (A–H), (453–464). San Diego, CA: Academic Press.

Reck, H-U. (2008). Im Gespraech. Retrieved from www.kultur-macht-europa.de/47.html.

Reckwitz, A. (2012). *Die Erfindung der Kreativitaet. Zum Prozess gesellschaftlicher Aesthetisierung.* Berlin, Germany: Suhrkamp Taschenbuch Wissenschaft.

Reichertz, J. (2012). Was bleibt vom goettlichen Funken? Ueber die Logik menschlicher Kreativitaet. In U. Göttlich and R. Kurt (Eds.), (63–78), op.cit.

DOI: 10.1057/9781137531223.0012

Rettig, D. (2010a). Alles ausser gewoehnlich: Wie sich Kreativitaet foerdern laesst. *Wirtschaftswoche (WIWO)*, July 23.

Rettig, D. (2010b). Lassen Sie keinen Stress entstehen – Der deutsche Kreativitaetsforscher Rainer Holm-Hadulla ueber die wichtigsten Regeln fuer mehr Einfallsreichtum. *Wirtschaftswoche (WIWO)*, July 26.

Reuter, M. (2011a). Invited Lecture/Power Point Presentation at the Deutsche Gesellschaft fuer Kreativitaet (German Creativity Association) in Mainz, Germany, May 28.

Reuter, M. (2011b). On Creativity. Paper presented at the International Conference of the International Journal of Arts and Sciences in Aix-En-Provence, France, June 7–10.

Reuter, M. (2015). The Crux with Creativity Research. In J. Preisz (Ed.), *2014 Jahrbuch der Kreativitaet*, (5–22). Koeln, Germany: Deutsche Gesellschaft fuer Kreativitaet.

Reuter, M., Panksepp, J., Schnabel N., Kellerhoff, N., Kempel, P., & Hennig, J. (2005). Personality and Biological Markers of Creativity. *European Journal of Personality*, 19(March, 2), 83–95.

Rhodes, M. (1961). An Analysis of Creativity. *Phi Delta Kappa*, 42, 350–310.

Richards, R. (1999a). Everyday Creativity. In M. Runco & S. Pritzker (Eds.), *Encyclopedia of Creativity*, Vol. 1 (A–H), (683–687). San Diego, CA: Academic Press.

Richards, R. (1999b). Four Ps of Creativity. In M. Runco & S. Pritzker (Eds.), *Encyclopedia of Creativity*, Vol. 1 (A–H), (733–741). San Diego, CA: Academic Press.

Richards, R. (Ed.). (2007). *Everyday Creativity and New Views of Human Nature. Psychological, Social and Spiritual Perspectives*. Washington, D.C.: American Psychological Association. Greenwich, Connecticut: Ablex Publishing Corporation.

Richards, S. E. (n.d.). Red-Hot Eco Moms. It's Only Natural to Want to Make the World a Better Place for Your Child. These 8 Green Women Did Something about It – From Designing Eco-Friendly Diapers to Creating an Environmentally Safe, Completely Ingestible Toy Cleaner. Retrieved from http://lifestyle.msn.com.

Richerson, P. & Boyd, R. (2005). *Not by Genes Alone. How Culture Transformed Human Evolution*. Chicago, IL: The University of Chicago Press.

Richman, J. (1997). Book Review: The Artist and the Emotional World: Creativity and Personality. *American Journal of Psychotherapy*, 51(Summer, 3), 449–450.

DOI: 10.1057/9781137531223.0012

Riedemann, K. (2011). Entschluesselt – Der Einstein-Code: Dem Geheimnis der Genies auf der Spur. *Hör Zu*, 20(5), 10–13.

Ritzer, G. (1996). *The McDonaldization of Society*. Thousand Oaks, CA: Pine Forge Press.

Ritzer, G. (n.d.). Retrieved from www.georgeritzer.com.

Robinson, K., Sir. (2001). *Out of Our Minds: Learning to Be Creative*. Oxford, England: Sparks Computer Solutions.

Robinson, K., Sir. (2010). *We are Educating People Out of Their Creativity*. TED: Ideas Worth Sharing, May 15.

Root-Bernstein, R. & Root-Bernstein, M. (2008). Imagine That! Annals of Ordinary and Extraordinary Genius. Teaching Creativity with TLC. Can Creativity Be Taught? One New Zealand School Shows How. *Psychology Today*, November 12.

Rose, F. (2002). The Father of Creative Destruction. Why Joseph Schumpeter Is Suddenly All the Rage in Washington. Retrieved from http://www.wired.com/wired/archive/10.03/schumpeter.html.

Ross, G. (2005). An Interview with Gregory Feist. Retrieved from http://www.americanscientist.org/bookshelf/pub/gregory-feist.

Runco, M. (1997). *The Creativity Research Handbook*, Vol. 1. Cresskill, NJ: Hampton Press.

Rusch, W. (2010). Kreativitaet – Eine Schluesselkompetenz fuer Gegenwart und Zukunft. Vortrag im Rahmen der Bildungsmesse didacta in Koeln. *Initiative hobby Kreativ*. Retrieved from www.initiative-hobbykreativ.de/kreativitaetsfoerderung3.html.

Saad, G. (2009). Cross-Cultural Differences in Creativity, July 13. Retrieved from *www.psychologytoday.com*.

Sales, A. & Fournier, M. (2007). *Knowledge, Communication and Creativity*. London, England: Sage Publications.

Sales, A., Fournier, M., & Sénéchal, Y. (2007). Knowledge, Communication, Reflexive Creativity and Social Change. In A. Sales and M. Fournier (3–30), op.cit.

Sawyer, R. K. (2006). *Explaining Creativity. The Science of Human Innovation*. Oxford, England: Oxford University Press.

Sawyer, R. K. (2007). *Group Genius, the Creative Power of Collaboration*. New York, NY: Basic Books.

Sawyer, R. K. (2009). *Keynote Lunch Reception*. Measuring Unique Studies Effectively (MUSE) Conference, February 8–11, Savannah, Georgia.

Sawyer, R. K. (2015). Preface: The Sociocultural Approach to Creativity. In V. P. Glăveanu, A. Gillespie, & J. Valsiner (Eds.), (xii–xiv), op.cit.

DOI: 10.1057/9781137531223.0012

Sawyer, R. K., John-Steiner, V., Moran, S., Sternberg, R., Feldman, D., Nakamura, J., & Csikszentmihalyi, M. (2003). *Creativity and Development*. New York, NY: Oxford University Press.

Schäfer, H. (2012). Kreativität und Gewohnheit. Ein Vergleich zwishen Praxistheorie und Pragmatismus. In U. Goettlich & R. Kurt (Eds.), *Kreativitaet und Improvisation. Soziologische Positionen* (17–43), Wiesbaden: Springer Fachmedien.

Schrader, C. (1993). Wo Soziologen fragen, wissen Physiker die Antwort. In *GEO Wissen*, (182–183), op.cit.

Schuldberg, D. (1999). Chaos Theory and Creativity. In M. Runco & S. Pritzker (Eds.), *Encyclopedia of Creativity*, Vol. 1 (A–H), (259–272). San Diego, CA: Academic Press.

Schumpeter. (2013). Back to the Drawing-Board: Design Companies Are Applying Their Skills to the Voluntary and Public Sectors. *The Economist*, July 6, 62.

Scriba, J. (1993). Auf dem Weg zum deterministischen Chaos ging der Laplacesche Daemon verloren. In *GEO Wissen*, (54–55), op.cit.

Seidman, S. (2010). *The Social Construction of Sexuality*. (2nd ed.). New York, NY: W. W. Norton & Company.

Segal, M. (2000). *Creativity and Personality Type: Tools for Understanding and Inspiring the Many Voices of Creativity*. Huntington Beach, CA: Telos Publications.

Selingo, J. (2012). Wanted: Better Employees. *The Chronicle of Higher Education*. Retrieved from *http://chronicle.com/blogs/next/2011/12/12/ wanted-better-employees/*.

Sennett, R. (2008). *The Craftsman*. New Haven, CN: Yale University Press.

Shellenbarger, S. (2010). A Box? Or a Spaceship? What Makes Kids Creative. *The Wall Street Journal*, December 15.

Shiu, S-C., Chien, H-O., Lee, M-H., & Chang, C-L. (2011). The Study of Brain Wave Change in Creative Thinking Process. Paper presented at the International Conference of the International Journal of Arts and Sciences in Aix-En-Provence, France, June 7–10.

Silver, D., Clark, T. N., & Graziuk, C. (2011). Scenes, Innovation, and Urban Development. In D. E. Andersson, Å. Andersson, & C. Mellander (Eds.), *Handbook of Creative Cities*, (229–258). Northampton, MA: Edward Elgar Publishing, Inc.

Simonton, D. K. (1999b). The Creative Society: Genius vis-à-vis the Zeitgeist. In A. Montuori & R. Purser (Eds.), *Social Creativity*, Vol. 1. (237–264). Cresskill, NJ: Hampton Press.

DOI: 10.1057/9781137531223.0012

Skillicorn, N. (2014). Creativity Is Not a Team Sport: Interview with Vincent Walsh. Retrieved from http://www.improvides. com/2014/03/24/creativity-team-sport-interview-vincent-walsh-prof-neuroscience-ucl/.

Smith, G. (2008). The Creative Personality in Search of a Theory. *Creativity Research Journal*, 20(4), 383–390.

Smith, G. & Carlsson, I. (2006). Creativity under the Northern Lights: Perspectives from Scandinavia. In J. Kaufman & R. Sternberg (Eds.), (202–234), op.cit.

Smith, R. (2008). Creativity in the Classroom: Igniting the Fire, Presentation at the 20th Southeastern Teaching of Psychology Conference held in Atlanta, GA.

Smith, S., Kerne, A., Koh, E., & Shah, J. (2009). The Development and Evaluation of Tools for Creativity. In A. Markman & K. Wood (Eds.), (128–154), op.cit.

Sommer, V. (1993). Das schoepferische Spiel. In *GEO Wissen,* (64–70), op.cit.

Spearman, C. (1927). *The Abilities of Man.* New York, NY: McMillan.

Spurlock, Morgan. (2009). *30 Days. Try Someone Else's Life on for Size.* An FX Original Series. Virgil Films.

Stam, H. (2001). Introduction: Social Constructionism and Its Critics. *Theory & Psychology*, 11(3), 291–296.

Stehr, N. (2007). Modern Societies as Knowledge Societies. In A. Sales & M. Fournier (Eds.), (31–42), op.cit.

Stepanossova, O. & Grigorenko, E. (2006). Creativity in Soviet-Russian Psychology. In J. Kaufman & R. Sternberg (Eds.), (235–269), op.cit.

Sternberg, R. (1985). *Beyond IQ: A Triarchic Theory of Human Intelligence.* New York, NY: Cambridge University Press.

Sternberg, R. (1999). *Handbook of Creativity.* Cambridge, England: Cambridge University Press.

Sternberg, R. & Lubart, T. (1999). The Concept of Creativity: Prospects and Paradigms. In R. Sternberg (Ed.), (3–15), op.cit.

Summers, J., Anandan, S., & Teegavarapu, S. (2009). Introduction of Design Enabling Tools: Development, Validation, and Lessons Learned. In A. Markman & K. Wood (Eds.), (195–215), op.cit.

Sutherland, S. (1995). What Mad Pursuit. Book Review of Ludwig, A. *The Price of Greatness. Nature,* June 15, 547–548.

Tanggaard, L. (2015). The Socio-Materiality of Creativity: A Case Study of the Creative Processes in Design Work. In V. P. Glăveanu, A. Gillespie, A., & J. Valsiner (Eds.), (110–124), op.cit.

DOI: 10.1057/9781137531223.0012

Tanner, D. (1997). *Total Creativity in Business and Industry.* New York, NY: Advanced Practical Thinking Training, Inc.

Tanner, J. (Ed.). (2003). *The Sociology of Art: A Reader.* London, England: Routledge.

Tepper, S. (2003). Creativity, Innovation and Society. Course Syllabus for Sociology 214 at Princeton University.

Thompson, C. (2013). Vaclav Smil. The Man Bill Gates Thinks You Should Be Reading. *Wired*, December, 72–79.

Thompson, N. (2002). May the Source Be with you. *The Washington Monthly*, 34 (7/8), 34–36.

Tönnesmann, J. (2009). Das groesste Problem der Menschheit ist armseliges, unkreatives Denken – Interview mit Edward de Bono. *Wirtschaftswoche (WIWO)*, February 12.

Torlina, J. (2011). *Working Class: Challenging Myths about Blue-Collar Labor.* Boulder, CO: Lynne Rienner Publishers.

Treffinger, D. (2000). *Creativity, Creative Thinking, and Critical Thinking: In Search of Definitions.* Ideas Capsules Series, Sarasota, FL: Center for Creative Learning.

Tudor, R. (2008). The Pedagogy of Creativity: Understanding Higher Order Capability Development in Design and Arts Education. *Proceedings of the 4th International Barcelona Conference on Higher Education*, Vol. 4. Barcelona, GUNI. Retrieved from http://www.guni-rmies.net.

Tversky, B. & Suwa, M. (2009). Thinking with Sketches. In A. Markman & K. Wood (Eds.), (75–84), op.cit.

United Nations. (2013). U.N. Development Programme. Retrieved from http://hdr.undp.org/en/.

Urry, J. (2007). Mobilities, Networks and Communities. In A. Sales, & M. Fournier (67–76), op.cit.

US National Debt. (2015). Retrieved from http://useconomy.about.com/od/monetarypolicy/f/Who-Owns-US-National-Debt.htm.

Valsiner, J., Glăveanu, V-P., & Gillespie, A. (2015). Editors' Introduction: Entering into the Creativity Zone, on the Border between the Mundane and the Monstrous. In V-P. Glăveanu, A. Gillespie and J. Valsiner (Eds.), (xv–xxiii), op.cit.

Vangkilde, K. T. (2012). Branding HUGO BOSS: An Anthropology of Creativity in Fashion. PhD thesis. University of Aarhus, Kopenhagen, Denmark. PhD Series no. 70. Faculty of Social Sciences, University of Copenhagen: Department of Anthropology.

DOI: 10.1057/9781137531223.0012

Vygotsky, L. (1971). *The Psychology of Art.* Cambridge, MA: MIT Press.
Wagoner, B. (2014). Creativity as Symbolic Transformation. In V. P. Glăveanu, A. Gillespie & J. Valsiner (Eds.), (16–30), op.cit.
Waytz, A. & Mason, M. (2013). Your Brain at Work. What a New Approach to Neuroscience Can Teach Us about Management. *Harvard Business Review,* July–August, 103–111.
Wehowsky, S. (1993). Die unvernuenftige Gesellschaft. *GEO Wissen* (152–161), op.cit.
Weisberg, R. (2009). On "Out-of-the-Box" Thinking in Creativity. In A. Markman & K. Wood (Eds.), (23–47), op.cit.
Weissman, K. (2001). Quiet: Grown-Ups at Play. *The O Magazine,* November, 220–222.
Whitehead, A. N. (1978). *Process and Reality: An Essay in Cosmology; Gifford Lectures Delivered in the University of Edinburgh during the Session 1927–1928.* (Corrected ed.). New York, NY: Free Press.
Whyte, M. (2009). Why Richard Florida's Honeymoon Is Over. *The Star.* Retrieved from http://www.thestar.com/news/insight/2009/06/27/why_richard_floridas_honeymoon_is_over.html.
Winner, L. (1993). Upon Opening the Black Box and Finding It Empty: Social Constructivism and the Philosophy of Technology. *Science, Technology and Human Values,* 18 (Summer, 3), 362–378.
Wozniak, S. (2006). *iWoz: Computer Geek to Cult Icon – How I Invented the Personal Computer, Co-founded Apple, and Had Fun Doing It.* New York, NY: Norton & Co.
Zimmer, D. (2001). Wenn Kreativitaet zu Innovationen fuehren soll: Gute neue Produkte werden zu Erfolgen. Daher muessen besonders mittelstaendische Unternehmen alles tun, um die kreativen *Potenziale ihrer Mitarbeiter freizusetzen. Harvard Business Manager,* 42–56.

DOI: 10.1057/9781137531223.0012

Name Index

DOI: 10.1057/9781137531223.0013

DOI: 10.1057/9781137531223.0013

DOI: 10.1057/9781137531223.0013

DOI: 10.1057/9781137531223.0013

DOI: 10.1057/9781137531223.0013

Subject Index

action theory approach to creativity, 33, 41
American Creativity Association, 4, 8
American Education, 10
American Psychological Association, 38
American values of creativity challenged, 53
Apple watch, 61
apprenticeships with highly skilled mentors, 62
AU Innovation Facilitators, 10
autopoiesis, 32
"average is over," *see* Cowen, 11
The Art Institute of Fort Lauderdale, 2, 65

behavioral traits desirable in employees, 28
biomimickry, 16, 31, 35
    biomimickry guild, 35
Bloom's Taxonomy of Learning objectives, 28
Bologna Process in Europe, 30
brain Wave Changes, *see* Shiu et al., 6

capacity for creativity by everyday people, 19
capitalism as a threat to creativity, 33
cell phone, 20
Center for Teaching, Research and Learning, 10

chaos theory, 8, 16, 31–32
CHI Conference, 2009, 6
children being "naturally" creative, 10, 28–29
collaborative webs, 23
commercial consulting/ consulting industry, 8, 16, 37–38
"communicamus, ergo sum" – we communicate, therefore I am, 45
comparison of students and employers/industry professionals, 71–74
concept trade-off exploration, 30
conferring of creative status socially, 63
Confucianism and creativity, 54–55
consulting firms, 8
corporate creativity training at the Center for Creative Leadership, 37
corporate ownership, decrease in, 24
creamus, ergo sumus or sumus, ergo creamus? 75
creative periods in cultures, 20
creativity
    annual revenue in Europe – *see* "European Community", 6
    creative consulting industry, 6
    creative class, *see* Richard Florida, 12

DOI: 10.1057/9781137531223.0014

DOI: 10.1057/9781137531223.0014

culture – *continued*
  cultural meaning systems, 45
  cultural psychologists, 77
  cultures of participation/social
    creativity, 36

The Daily Creative Food Company, 2
democratization of creativity, 18
decline in creativity as a result of rote
  learning and standardized testing,
  29
demioergoi, i.e., public producers, 32
design enablers, 30
design spiral, 35
design thinking, 16
design thinking for social innovation,
  32, 34–35
Deutsche Gesellschaft für Kreativität, 8
differences between Eastern and
  Western conceptions of creativity,
  53
discourses on creativity as preferences,
  58
Discovery Channel, 6
domain gatekeepers, 19
d.school at Stanford University, 35

economic theory of creativity, 16, 32
efficiency, the virtue of the
  "Organization Man", 79
emic and etic research methodologies,
  52, 81
employees' creative potential, 18
employers and industry professionals,
  67–70
engineers' perception of control vs
  freedom in creative work, 18
epigenetic development, 80
European Commission, 6
European Community, 14
European critique of American
  exclusive quantitative
  methodologies, 52
  see also "North American bias", 52
everyday and social creativity theories,
  16, 18

external confirmation through
  competent experts, 63
exploratory study, 65

fabrication of creativity, 78
Flow, 61
Flynn effect, see Bronson and
  Merryman, 10
focus groups, 65
four Ps of creativity, 18
Food Network USA, 6
fostering creativity in the classroom, 28
French Creativity Association (CREA), 8

"gainful employment", 14
Gardner's Ten-Year Rule, 30
gatekeepers, 19
genius, 25, 33
  strong genetic component, running
    in families, 25
GEO Science Magazine, 9
German Cultural Minister, 6
German Idealism, 24
glorification of creative individuals, 25
groups as sources of creativity, 23

"he, I and we paradigm", 33
history of craft, 17
history of creativity in psychology, 38
HOK architectural corporation, 35
Home and Garden Television, 59
homo creativus, 75
HR's Workplace Learning and
  Development Team, 10
Human Development Report, 2013 –
  see United Nations
human nature and creativity, 58–59

IBM Global CEO study, 75
IDEO, 24, 34–35
ideologies and their social contexts, 62
imagination, power of, 17
I-paradigm, 18
Inc. Guidebook, 7
individualized and technologized
  Western industrial societies, 21

DOI: 10.1057/9781137531223.0014

DOI: 10.1057/9781137531223.0014

DOI: 10.1057/9781137531223.0014

DOI: 10.1057/9781137531223.0014

CPI Antony Rowe
Eastbourne, UK
March 31, 2019